Total Depravity Decently & In Order:
Sermons from an Ongoing Reformation

George W. Chapman III

Total Depravity Decently & In Order: Sermons from an Ongoing Reformation

ISBN: Softcover 978-1-946478-20-7

Copyright © 2017 by George W. Chapman III

All rights reserved. No part of this book may be reproduced or transmitted in any form or by any means, electronic or mechanical, including photocopying, recording, or by any information storage and retrieval system, without permission in writing from the publisher.

To order additional copies of this book, contact:

Parson's Porch Books
1-423-475-7308
www.parsonsporch.com

Parson's Porch Books is an imprint of **Parson's Porch & Book Publishers** in Cleveland, Tennessee, which has double focus. We focus on the needs of creative writers who need a professional publisher to get their work to market, **&** we also focus on the needs of others by sharing our profits with those who struggle in poverty to meet their basic needs of food, clothing, shelter and safety.

*Total Depravity Decently & In Order:
Sermons from an Ongoing Reformation*

For Myra

Table of Content

Introduction 9
Great Expectations 17
The Sum of the Parts 25
A Tough Crowd 31
Pick of the Litter 38
Letter of the Law 43
Forced Perspectives 49
Place Your Bets 55
Topsy-Turvy 61
Promises, Promises 67
The Good Stuff 71
Ready or Not 77
What Goes Up 83
All You Can Eat 94
A Eulogy for Uncle George 101
Letting Go 106
You Break It, You Buy It 112
Famous Last Words 118
Direct from the Source 123
Déjà Vu All Over Again 129
All Good Things 135
Sibling Rivalry 141
Dividing Lines 147
The Unkindest Cut 154
Forget Me Not 159
Moving Day 165
Just Desserts 171
No Man's Land 177

Introduction

Truth be told, I don't really know why I'm a pastor. Let's face it, on paper, I wouldn't consider myself the ideal candidate. I don't exactly crave the spotlight. I'm definitely not an extrovert. Any ability I have to initiate conversation has been carefully and awkwardly cultivated over the last so many years through a process of trial and error. As it happens, I maxed out the "Thinking" scale of my Myers-Briggs personality inventory, so I admit how certain feelings and attitudes can sometimes escape my notice. I'm not the most spiritual person in the world. I'm not part of some multigenerational family legacy. (I think I may have had a great-great-grandfather who was a pastor, but I'm sure he was Baptist!) I'm not particularly well-connected within the Presbyterian Church (USA), nor do I serve a large, influential congregation. Although I find polity fascinating, I have little threshold for church politics. Why someone like myself would publicly and professionally invite the scrutiny of others, I have no earthly idea.

When I think about it, I really have only two things going for me. First, I look the part: Tall, lanky, cleans up moderately well, looks good in black—it turns out, that can get you far in this business! The second is this annoying sense of call. It sounds almost crazy to say, but for some reason unbeknownst to me, I believe the words that are coming out of my mouth each Sunday morning—words of grace, words of justice, words of encouragement, words of redemption and hope. Words are important to me, and I figure, if I don't at least believe them, I can't really expect anyone else to, either. Maybe the "why" will continue to prove elusive, but at the end of the day, a pastor is what…or perhaps more accurately…*who* I am. And in a strange kind of way, the fact that I can't rationally explain it only confirms why it had to be me, and not someone else who might fare better by the numbers.

What a strange profession! Think about it: Every Sunday I get up to speak before a group of people who are interested in what I must say! It boggles the mind! If you take away the fancy robe and the pulpit and placed me out on the street-corner somewhere, people would likely regard me as insane. And yet inside the walls of a church, not only is this perfectly acceptable, people pay me to do it! Of course, being a pastor can be emotionally and spiritually demanding, but it really is the greatest job in the world. I get to paid to learn. I get paid to play. I get paid to form genuine relationships, pray for folks in need and eat homemade dinners. I get paid to do some small good in the world! What an amazing concept! Despite the many vagaries presented by theology and religion, I find myself completely in my element.

In the Fall of 2016, I had the honor and the privilege of auditing a class at Union, taught by noted seminary president and all-around awesome biblical scholar, Dr. Brian K. Blount. The class entitled, "Cultural Interpretation of the New Testament", sought to examine scripture from a variety of social and cultural perspectives which students may not have considered before. For the mid-term, Dr. Blount challenged us to examine our own cultural lens through which we encountered New Testament texts. For the purposes of this introduction, I thought this might make a good place to start, to identify the main points of intersection which exert their influence when I personally engage scripture, those being (1) myself, (2) my congregation and (3) the text itself.

Myself: I am under no illusion that, historically (and contemporarily) speaking, I belong to a privileged group. My upper-middle class suburbanite upbringing afforded me many opportunities which may not have come about otherwise. I admit how I have not had to endure the same prejudices that others have encountered while trying to have their voices heard within the larger conversation of faith. I acknowledge the extent to which, over the last one thousand years or so, the lens of scriptural interpretation has been almost exclusively white, Western European and male. It's also impossible to deny the extent to which scriptural interpretation has been—and still is—used and abused to disenfranchise persons from full participation in church and society.

Although I may appear from all external measures as the poster-child for the status quo, I also acknowledge how I belong to this radical, revolutionary Christian tradition of faith that is particularly called to be the voice of protest injustice and oppression wherever it manifests itself. Through this "Reformed, always reforming" tradition, in its purest and noblest expression, the community of faith seeks to exist as a witness to the world where all voices are welcome—dare I say, necessary—in its life and mission.

Congregation: In 2015, I accepted a call as pastor of First Presbyterian Church of Waynesboro, Virginia, a small city located in the heart of the Shenandoah Valley at the foot of the Blue Ridge Mountains. Like many churches, my congregation is being forced to adapt to a new reality as religious attitudes in the United States continue to evolve. Presently, its membership is but a small fraction of what it was in former times. Trends of decline reached a crisis point after the previous pastor attempted to lead the congregation out of the PC(USA) due to the denomination's increasingly progressive views on inclusiveness, as expressed through ordination and marriage. The result of these efforts was a split in the congregation which had a dramatic effect on the collective psyche. This experience, perhaps more than anything, informs First Presbyterian's identity as a faith community moving forward.

Although I would hardly consider our church to be a bastion of liberal theology, they have made great sacrifices to establish themselves as a more inclusive, more welcoming body of faith in the local community. Indeed, two LGBTQ couples have since joined our church and become active participants in its life and leadership. Naturally, there is considerable uncertainty over what kind of church they want to become, however, recent history has taught them what kind of church they *do not* want to be!

Text: I consider my views on scripture to be in keeping with this radical, reforming tradition of faith which emphasizes the exercise of critical thought in the interpretation of biblical scriptures. I proceed with an understanding of what scripture *is* (the living Word of God), but also what it *is not* (a rule book, a history book). Whether we are talking about gospels, epistles, prophets or psalms, I affirm scripture to be the story of the relationship shared between God and God's people, and as such, story plays a central role in how I encounter scripture.

The exercise of critical thought in the interpretation of scripture involves considerable questions when engaging a passage: What is happening in the story? How does the passage speak to the need of the church at the time in which it was written? How does a given passage operate in the context of the overall narrative? How does the scripture work in the context of the whole of scripture? Who are the principal characters? What voices do they represent in their own cultural context? Who might they represent in ours? What are the theological issues present in the passage? How does this text affirm what I believe? What do I find personally challenging or troubling? Where is the point of crisis in the story? What is the source of creative tension found within scripture that forces the reader outside of their reality and into God's reality?

Consistent engagement with biblical texts has caused my personal views on scripture to evolve significantly throughout the years. I view scripture as an ongoing conversation emerging from among the people of God. Scripture frequently illustrates how God speaks through the wonderful diversity of creation, and as parts of that creation, the same principle also applies to human beings. Since the writers of scripture are struggling with their human limitations to conceptualize divine mysteries of redemption and salvation, such matters cannot be easily conceptualized by means of written communication. (A medium which began as drawings etched upon cave walls proves poorly equipped for the task.) Nevertheless, despite these limitations, their conversation can help guide our own. And if we affirm the Holy Spirit to be present during this ongoing conversation, then it stands to reason that the more voices we can include, the more Spirit may be heard with greater clarity and emphasis.

To discover the context in which these three points intersect, I tried coming up with themes that might be particularly relevant to the life of my congregation. However, given the body of work which I accumulated throughout the years, a more constructive approach (or more accurately, a more "deconstructive" approach) might be to reflect upon themes which appear to manifest themselves in my sermons and lessons most frequently. Those are:

Creation: I owe much to Terrence Fretheim, whose Westminster John Knox commentary on Exodus opened my eyes to seeing scripture as the story of God's *ongoing* act of creation. Applying this to the whole of scripture challenges the reader to see how the hand of God is present in the narrative. Moreover, a theology of creation forces the reader to consider how we live and act as parts of this greater story. What does it mean to be a creation of God? How do we see others as fellow creations of God? Acknowledging God's ongoing act of creation is crucial if we are to liberate ourselves from narrow and exclusionary, "us vs. them", "Christ vs. culture" theologies.

Justice & Judgment: These are other important topics which a 21st century "Feelgood Christianity" prefers to neglect. Although we certainly affirm the sovereignty of God's forgiveness and mercy, we cannot ignore the reality of God's judgment revealed through maladjusted relationships and broken societies. Calls for justice and reconciliation are just as relevant now as they were 2,000 years ago. Where today do we hear prophetic voices calling wayward nations and peoples back to repentance? It may be wise to listen…

Predestination: Free will is overrated. (That's right…I said it!) While traditional doctrines of predestination must be understood considering historical and social circumstances, I still feel it is important for the church of our age to affirm the sovereignty of God over our world and over our lives. This applies to our understanding of scripture, the foremost lesson being, *what God wants, God gets*. Besides, how we are predestined is significantly less important than what we are predestined to as the children of God [Rom. 8:29, Eph. 1:5, I Thess. 5:9].

Total Depravity: This is another one of those Reformation principles which people today find difficult to stomach, that idea that we are sinners in a broken world who are completely dependent upon God for our salvation. We so terribly profess our innocence, and that, 'we' are, 'good' while, 'they' are, 'bad'. Scripture, however, would appear to offer us a different perspective on the matter, with human characters who simultaneously possess both good and bad tendencies. Early Hebrew patriarchs such as, Noah, Abraham and Jacob were flawed and imperfect people, as were David and Jesus' disciples. Nevertheless, despite their human weaknesses, God could affect meaningful transformation through them. Original sin is only the beginning of this story of faith and redemption. Depravity is not the end to which we are condemned, but it marks the beginning of renewed hope.

Life & Death: "In life and in death we belong to God," affirms *A Brief Statement of Faith* from the Presbyterian Church (USA)'s *Book of Confessions*. It remains vital that we place trust and hope in a God who is present with us throughout the entirety of our lives, and that death is but a part of life's natural cycle. This does not merely apply to our individual lives, but our collective life as an ever-evolving, ever-adapting faith community. The church is always changing; new expressions and institutions are born, while others are laid to rest—it's the way things have always been. Mortality informs us how our responsibility as the church assumes a greater urgency if we are going to make the best possible use of the time and gifts we have been allotted. That is why scripture consistently warns against complacency and apathy, while perseverance and preparedness are regarded as the highest of Christian virtues. Each day presents us with new opportunities to love and to serve the Lord.

Community: It may be a symptom of the age in which we live, but too often scripture is interpreted through an individual lens. However, the clear majority of scripture is addressed directly to the whole community of faith. How does the message of scripture change, when we rescue it from the personal realm and apply it to the life of the whole? How does our understanding of discipleship altered, when we come to understand ourselves as part of something greater than ourselves? How are popular standards for morality and piety challenged when we are all held to account for our collective failure to seek God's justice and righteousness, either as a church or as a nation? In scripture, strength is found in numbers, and no one ever gets left behind.

Love: I often (half-jokingly) say, "I don't feel the need to preach with consistency because the Bible doesn't preach with consistency." And whereas I believe this to be true to a certain extent when considering various and sundry social and religious issues, I do feel the need to walk that statement back a step or two. The Bible does indeed preach a consistent message of love, because that is really what the story is all about! Love for God and for neighbor provides the context for every word in scripture, therefore, if we are not using scripture in a loving manner, then we have missed the point of it, and the purposes for which it was given.

The church of the 20th century was defined by ecumenism, with churches and denominations coming together to celebrate what we share as brothers and sisters in Christ. Ecumenism is a noble end which will continue to play an important role in the future direction of the Christian faith. However, equally important for the 21st century will be acknowledging those principles which make us distinct as a community of believers. A strong historical and theological tradition with its emphasis on inclusiveness and freedom of conscience will be a strong asset in the years to come. In the spirit of such, I have compiled these sermons as part confession, part apology and part manifesto for the Reformed Tradition of our time and place. But any delusions of grandeur aside, I just hope it's a fun read and gives you something to think about.

Well anyway, I've rambled long enough, but this should offer some sense of where I'm coming from as one voice within this grand conversation of Christian faith. Finally, as a disclaimer, please bear in mind that I am a pastor, and not a theologian or a biblical scholar. I do have a fine appreciation for those disciplines, but like so many other things, I prefer to leave such matters in more qualified hands than my own. Consequently, I am not above the occasional exegetical leap; sometimes I land on my feet, sometimes not so much. Neither am I naïve enough to expect everyone to agree with everything I say. If anything, my hope for any sermon is that it may act as a catalyst for conversation, which in turn, can serve as a basis for mutual understanding.

Truth will bear itself out, eventually. But in the meantime, take my words for what they are worth, and as always, let the buyer beware!

Grace & Peace,

George

My first sermon at First Presbyterian Church of Waynesboro was delivered while I was still pastor of nearby Buena Vista Presbyterian Church. I was tasked by a planning team to preach the sermon at the August meeting of the Shenandoah Presbytery, for a service which, "celebrates our Reformed, always reforming, tradition". The site of the meeting was an act of solidarity with the congregation of First Presbyterian, which had only recently voted to remain within the PC(USA) after the previous pastor attempted to lead them into another denomination. The result of that vote caused a rift in the congregation, whereby the pastor, the associate pastor, most the session and half the congregation left to form their own church. What remained was an older group of traditional Presbyterians, whose membership rolls had been gutted to the point of near-unsustainability. This new uncertainty was (and still is) the source of much anxiety as the church moves forward. Nevertheless, although there is considerable apprehension, there is also an even greater hope that God is still working through them and among them. I intended this sermon to act as an assurance for a church which has always been dynamic and transforming, even from the very start.

Great Expectations

14 Then Jesus, filled with the power of the Spirit, returned to Galilee, and a report about him spread through all the surrounding country. 15 He began to teach in their synagogues and was praised by everyone.

16 When he came to Nazareth, where he had been brought up, he went to the synagogue on the Sabbath day, as was his custom. He stood up to read, 17 and the scroll of the prophet Isaiah was given to him. He unrolled the scroll and found the place where it was written:

18 'The Spirit of the Lord is upon me,

19 because he has anointed me

20 to bring good news to the poor.
    He has sent me to proclaim release to the captives
    and recovery of sight to the blind,
    let the oppressed go free,

21 to proclaim the year of the Lord's favor.'

20And he rolled up the scroll, gave it back to the attendant, and sat down. The eyes of all in the synagogue were fixed on him. 21Then he began to say to them, 'Today this scripture has been fulfilled in your hearing.' 22All spoke well of him and were amazed at the gracious words that came from his mouth. They said, 'Is not this Joseph's son?' 23He said to them, 'Doubtless you will quote to me this proverb, "Doctor, cure yourself!" And you will say, "Do here also in your home town the things that we have heard you did at Capernaum."' 24And he said, 'Truly I tell you, no prophet is accepted in the prophet's home town. 25But the truth is, there were many widows in Israel in the time of Elijah, when the heaven was shut up for three years and six months, and there was a severe famine over all the land; 26yet Elijah was sent to none of them except to a widow at Zarephath in Sidon. 27There were also many lepers in Israel in the time of the prophet Elisha, and none of them was cleansed except Naaman the Syrian.' 28When they heard this, all in the synagogue were filled with rage. 29They got up, drove him out of the town, and led him to the brow of the hill on which their town was built, so that they might hurl him off the cliff. 30But he passed through the midst of them and went on his way.

Luke 4:14-30 (NRSV)

You don't know how disappointed I was the day that my parents informed me that there were no dinosaurs. As a boy, I had a great many dinosaur books, dinosaur toys and other assorted dinosaur-related paraphernalia, and I would have spent countless hours scribbling prehistoric scenes of the great beasts upon the surplus of used office papers which my dad brought home from work. My family even visited the Natural History Museum in Washington D.C. to see the amazing collection of fossils and bones, but it never occurred to me for one moment that there weren't any dinosaurs left! I figured, surely there must be at least one zoo somewhere in the world with one or two on display. It's not even like I was asking for something exotic like a Tyrannosaur or even a Brachiosaur, just maybe even something slightly more "pedestrian" like a Triceratops or Iguanodon. Nevertheless, upon learning the truth, I was crushed and crestfallen, the dreams of childhood savagely eviscerated by the cold and unforgiving teeth of natural selection.

No matter what age people are, no one ever enjoys having their bubble burst. Just ask the people of Nazareth. Never are people quite as angry as when they have their expectations ingloriously dashed by circumstance—or worse, by someone else. And so, it is in the fourth chapter of Luke's gospel that we bear witness as a young rabbi returns to his home town in triumph. Imagine the peoples' excitement to hear the Word from a local boy who has already made quite a reputation for himself in and around nearby Galilee. ("Ooh, let's go hear Joseph and Mary's son speak in church today…Won't that be nice?" "I guess so…but I'll tell you right now, he had better have us out of there by noon!")

Many here can certainly appreciate the pressures that are placed upon a young pastor, especially for one who comes to preach before the hometown crowd. They can be an intimidating lot. And I would imagine the people who gathered in the synagogue back in Jesus' time were pretty much like any congregation that one might find today. Each brought with them their own personal interests, but they also carried with them great concern for the tradition of their faith. And as Jesus made his way through the excited crowd that morning, there were certainly many who were quick to share their opinions on such lofty matters, or offer their diagnosis on what exactly is ailing the present state of religion.

Now believe it or not, such concern is a good thing, you want people to be invested and engaged in the life of the church, but it is quite a lot to place upon the shoulders of any individual, even those of Jesus Christ. "How do we get young people into the synagogue?"

"How are we going to compete with all the crowds at the circus or the theatre on the Sabbath?" "How can we define ourselves as a congregation?" "How can we grow the church?" "Hey, Jesus, what are *you* going to do to grow the church?" Now, these are all truly worthy concerns which people wrestle with on a regular basis; if we truly loved our faith, we would be foolish not to have them. The trouble for the people of Nazareth, however, is that Jesus does in fact offer them a remedy for the future of their faith. Unfortunately, it is medicine his fellow Nazoreans find too bitter to swallow.

As it happens, the first half of this story goes extremely well for Jesus. He enters into the synagogue on the Sabbath and reads the scroll from the prophet Isaiah (always a popular choice among the locals), punctuated by a rather bold statement, *"Today this scripture has been fulfilled in your hearing."* And perhaps this young rabbi should have had the good sense to stop there, for as Luke describes, the people, *"were amazed at the gracious words that came from his mouth"*. The synagogue was no doubt abuzz with glowing reviews of the message they had just received, and began to speculate wildly about all the wonderful things that this young rabbi could do for their congregation for the future. There is little doubt that if Jesus just set up shop here, many people would come from far around to hear this charismatic preacher speak within these very walls. Jesus could settle down, raise a family and make a comfortable living as a leader in the local synagogue. The future was bright for Jesus of Nazareth. Yes, the sky was the limit for this promising young rabbi, provided of course, he had the presence of mind to keep his opinions to himself!

Yet Jesus quickly spoils the party by saying, "Yes, you may endeavor to grow the church and you may want to grow in faith, but this means that much will be required. You will have to set yourself free from moral judgment and self-righteous indignation. You are going to have to welcome in a lot of people who you might not have considered before. As you know, the prophet Elijah was sent to a widow in a foreign land; Elisha healed a diseased adversary and a killer of men. If the Spirit of the Lord is truly upon you, you will have to reach out to the poor, the lame, the widow and the outcast. You are going to have to open your doors to the alien, the enemy, the unclean—all those who allegedly live outside the covenant of God's promises. No longer can you cling to this former idea that people should be in church simply because you expect them to be there. No longer do you have the luxury of picking and choosing the company you keep. Justice begins at home, and if you are going to be the people who God has called you to be, you will to have to start by going out of your way to welcome all people into your midst."

You can almost imagine several seconds of stunned silence as the weight of Jesus' message begins to sink in. Once it does, this declaration *infuriates* the people of Nazareth—so much so, that Luke states that they, *"were filled with rage"* and threatened to throw their native son off a cliff! "What do you mean; welcome strangers and outcasts into these sacred walls? Are you mad? You've got some nerve! We don't have to take this from the likes of you!" The people of Nazareth expected Jesus to just speak sunshine and daisies to thank them for their generous support of his ministry. They expected Jesus to affirm that they were God's chosen and their enemies were destined for God's judgment. They expected Jesus to use his miraculous abilities to exclusively serve *them*, to cure *them* all their ills and relieve *them* of *their* many burdens. And yet the prescription that Jesus offers is the very one which they cannot stomach. Thus, this once promising young rabbi becomes driven away from his very home. By showing the courage to declare the honest-to-God Word, Jesus turns his back on a life of comfort and security so that he might venture out into the world to that place where God was calling him.

Both then, as with now, people place a lot of expectations on Jesus, and do not respond too well when he displays the audacity to dash them. And like the people of Nazareth, it seems like people today prove all-too willing to only listen to half of what Jesus says, seeking an answer to that eternal question, "Hey, what's in it for me?" Now, I certainly don't want to diminish the importance of human need in our Christian experience, after all, we all come to Jesus because we need something, but if we only come to Jesus solely concerned about our own personal needs, then we miss out on a significant part of the message. No matter if they are spiritual or physical, *our needs are important to God*, but the urgency of such personal matters frequently causes people to lose sight of the needs of others.

I mean, simply venture into to the "Christian" section of any bookstore nowadays, and browse the titles on the shelf, and you might have a difficult time differentiating it from the "Self-Help" section. It would appear as if Christian faith has become more and more centered upon what God can do to improve our individual lives, as if the gospel was a series of handy little tips designed to make our lives better by curing that which ails us. *How to Argue Like Jesus: Learning Persuasion from History's Greatest Communicator; Made to Crave: Satisfying Your Deepest Desire with God, Not Food; Called to Lead: 26 Leadership Lessons from the Life of the Apostle Paul; Lady in Waiting: Becoming God's Best While Waiting for Mr. Right*. Now we may chuckle and laugh, but this is what's out there! When people have genuine questions about faith and what it means to be Christian, this is what people see! Although perhaps well intended, such musings show a tendency to offer priority to our individual yearnings rather than balancing them with our collective obligation to live as God's people.

And as a pastor in the Protestant tradition, I find it somewhat disheartening to look out across the American religious landscape today. You see wonderful and welcoming congregations in towns and communities that struggle to keep the doors open and the lights on. You count the declining numbers in your own pews and your own denomination, while watching as people flock in great numbers to celebrity preachers and personalities who cater exclusively to our individual cravings. You turn on the television to see stadium-sized mega-churches filled with wide-eyed people desperately waiting to hear tales of the many rewards that God has in store for them. You hear Christians proudly testify about accepting Jesus Christ as their *personal* Lord and Savior, rather than the Lord and Savior of the entire world! You ride across the interstate in your car and see huge warehouses with makeshift steeples and great billboards outside that promise, "Come inside! Discover contentment! Be fulfilled! Find *peace!*"

But **NO**! In a world of poverty and disparity, I will not be content! I don't want fulfillment while people remain oppressed or marginalized, or are held captive to fear and violence! If injustice persists in this world, I refuse to have peace! If the Spirit of the Lord is truly upon us, then we must once again lend our voice to boldly proclaim the Lord's favor. Our Christian tradition the Presbyterian tradition was forged in the fires of *protest* and *discontent.* Our ancestors faithfully took up their cross against tyranny and exploitation. We openly defied the will of kings, popes and emperors for the sake of human dignity as we reclaimed our voice within Christ's church. We resisted Crusades and Inquisitions for the cause of God's justice and righteousness, confident in the knowledge that *these* are the things that are needed in this world and that *these* are the things that are demanded of all God's people. Our Protestant heritage affirms that God has great expectations of us, and it is not just self-help, but the help of all people that has been our calling since the very beginning in Nazareth.

Jesus reminds his followers that welcoming others can indeed be a radical act—a form of protest all the self-indulgent claims of those who would enslave faith to serve personal ambition. Now that's an unpopular message, even to this day. As Christ's disciples and members of one body, we are to graciously embrace all people into our midst, and yet we notice how all too often cries for justice and reconciliation fall upon deaf ears, because people still assume, "Well, there's nothing in it for me!" People display a habit of just wanting to hear the first half of the story; we always want to hear what the Lord will do *for* us rather than what God demands *of* us. Weighed against the fast and flashy face of a feel-good Christianity, it appears as if mainstream Protestantism is little more than an obtuse assortment of giant, bloated dinosaurs lumbering their way to certain extinction.

Therefore, many people are convinced…*convinced*…that Protestant churches must become more like what is "popular" if we wish to survive—that the young people and families will come flowing back for things as simple as PowerPoint projections and rock-and-roll praise bands, "contemporary" worship services, book clubs and self-help seminars. Such things can be valuable tools of faith expression, but these external trappings, no matter how grand or well-intended, are ultimately for nothing if the people in our pews fail to feel welcome or valued. If innovation comes at the cost of the justice which God requires, if we seek to appeal to people's senses rather than their sensibilities, if we feel pressured to warp ourselves into something we're not or compromise tradition for the sake of what is popular, then we are being disingenuous to ourselves and to the God whom we claim to serve. If we cannot live and worship and serve one another openly, in truth and with sincerity among friend and stranger alike, well, I'll be honest with you—I, like Jesus, would prefer to take my chances out on the road.

It is disappointing to say that still to this day, I have never gotten to see a real, live dinosaur. But you know, there are many biologists and paleontologists out there who make the claim that the dinosaurs never actually went extinct. There is a prevailing theory that, over time, the dinosaurs grew smaller and more mobile. It took a while, but eventually, they would shed their rough scales in favor of colorful feathers which they would use to take flight into the sky. They would adapt to life in a new world, and it is from on high that these creatures live on to enjoy a different perspective on God's creation, unbound by forces which hold other creatures down. Thus, we may find them as they follow the seasons, soaring among the clouds or darting between the trees, building nests, caring for their young, and going wherever the winds might carry them next.

Perhaps there is a lesson somewhere in there of what it means to be the church. Birds of a feather flock together, after all. That Spirit which calls us together into this radical community of faith is the same Spirit that is constantly forming and reforming us according to God's purposes. There are certainly people in the world and in our communities who would eagerly share our beliefs and our traditions; there are those who value evangelism by example, community in conscience, mission through mercy. There are many out there who already believe in such things, it's just a question of whether we will have the courage to speak up and speak out, making us visible by placing ourselves above the crowd, so that others can find us should the need arise. Perhaps if we spread our wings wide enough, the Holy Spirit will lift us up to carry us to those strange and mysterious places where our Lord calls. Given enough time, if we can manage to fly high and well enough on our own, then by the grace of God, we never really must worry about ever being let down.

We don't have to pretend to be something different than what we are.

We don't even have to be what we once were.

All we must ever be is the church.

Blessing and glory and wisdom and thanksgiving and honor and power and might be to our God forever and ever. Amen.

In the spring of 2015, I officially accepted a call to be pastor of First Presbyterian Church in Waynesboro, Virginia. What brought me to this congregation was the great courage they displayed by taking a stand against the divisive rhetoric which has taken its toll on the Presbyterian Church (USA) over the last two decades. I am of the mind that our denomination, and indeed the whole one, holy, catholic and apostolic church, will have great need of such courage as we accept the challenges of the future. In that sense, I believe First Presbyterian to be a prototype congregation for church of the 21st century: smaller, older, and more inclusive, with an even greater community focus, both among our pews and out in the world. Once all the dust of conflict has settled, how do we move forward as Christ's church? How can we rediscover our voice within the greater chorus of Christianity? Such questions describe the very nature, and the challenge, of the Resurrection.

Given First Presbyterian's recent history, I uncharacteristically ventured off-lectionary for my inaugural Sunday in the pulpit. The prophet Ezekiel seemed particularly well-suited for the task at hand.

The Sum of the Parts
June 14, 2015

1 The hand of the Lord came upon me, and he brought me out by the spirit of the Lord and set me down in the middle of a valley; it was full of bones. ²He led me all round them; there were very many lying in the valley, and they were very dry. ³He said to me, 'Mortal, can these bones live?' I answered, 'O Lord God, you know.' ⁴Then he said to me, 'Prophesy to these bones, and say to them: O dry bones, hear the word of the Lord. ⁵Thus says the Lord God to these bones: I will cause breath to enter you, and you shall live. ⁶I will lay sinews on you, and will cause flesh to come upon you, and cover you with skin, and put breath in you, and you shall live; and you shall know that I am the Lord.'

7 So I prophesied as I had been commanded; and as I prophesied, suddenly there was a noise, a rattling, and the bones came together, bone to its bone. ⁸I looked, and there were sinews on them, and flesh had come upon them, and skin had covered them; but there was no breath in them. ⁹Then he said to me, 'Prophesy to the breath, prophesy, mortal, and say to the breath: Thus, says the Lord God: Come from the four winds, O breath, and breathe upon these slain, that they may live.' ¹⁰I prophesied as he commanded me, and the breath came into them, and they lived, and stood on their feet, a vast multitude.

11 Then he said to me, 'Mortal, these bones are the whole house of Israel. They say, "Our bones are dried up, and our hope is lost; we are cut off completely." ¹²Therefore prophesy, and say to them, Thus says the Lord God: I am going to open your graves, and bring you up from your graves, O my people; and I will bring you back to the land of Israel.¹³And you shall know that I am the Lord, when I open your graves, and bring you up from your graves, O my people. ¹⁴I will put my spirit within you, and you shall live, and I will place you on your own soil; then you shall know that I, the Lord, have spoken and will act, says the Lord.'

Ezekiel 37:1-14 (NRSV)

Among the prophets of the Old Testament, the prophet Ezekiel stands alone. Unlike other prophets such as Jeremiah or Isaiah, who boldly declare pronouncements and judgments upon the kingdoms of the world, with Ezekiel, we as the reader find ourselves essentially, "along for the ride" in this spiritual journey, so that through the prophet's words, we see as he sees and we experience what he experiences. We (like the prophet) struggle to make sense of the surreal and mysterious images which transpire before our very eyes. During his story, Ezekiel is offered a series of visions by the Lord which describe the humiliation of Jerusalem at the hands of Judah's enemies. They are images of complete destruction, ultimate devastation, an entire people laid low and humiliated in the worst possible way, and yet, at the same time, the words of the prophet will eventually sow the seeds of a new hope and a new reality of life in true relationship with God.

Our scripture lesson today represents the third of four visions offered to Ezekiel by the Lord. In this scene that unfolds before us, we are presented with a valley full of dry bones, the skeletal remains of countless individuals strewn about the landscape as far as the eye can see. Often in our liturgy, we speak metaphorically of the, "Valley of the Shadow of Death", but this is where Ezekiel literally finds himself, and it is truly unsettling indeed. It is here in this valley where a vast multitude lie dead and forgotten; so much time has passed that not even the stench of death remains. These bones now serve little purpose in the world other than to serve as a warning for others who may consider walking the same fateful path. This valley is presented to us as a place absent of life and hope, and so therefore, we are taken aback when the voice of the Lord comes upon the prophet to ask a simple question, *"Mortal, can these bones live?"*

Now strangely enough, the prophet finds himself in kind of a predicament. On the one hand, he has already borne witness to the majesty and power of the Lord first hand. He knows that the God is the Lord of life, the very One who separated the waters of creation and fashioned humankind from the clay of the earth. Ezekiel is a faithful person, he understands all of this, and yet this scene that now lies before him is so completely devoid of even the slightest hint of vitality, he cannot quite conceive of how life could ever possibly be restored. I mean, this kind of makes sense, don't you think? Dead people don't just rise from the grave! On the one hand, we also consider ourselves to be a faithful people—we too affirm our faith in trust in God who is the giver of life and the creator of all things, and yet we routinely see on the news or across our communities places which would appear to be without hope. We witness devastation which defies the imagination and this makes us wonder…we wonder where God can be during all this inconceivable misery, or perhaps we may wonder if the Lord is even present at all!

And so, caught in this pickle, Ezekiel's response avoids the question altogether. *"O Lord God, you know…"* On the surface his words sound faithful and hopeful, and yet somehow tinged with a yellow hue of doubt. We assume that Ezekiel's faith is being tested, but we soon discover that this passage is not even about him or us. It is not about mortal faith, or lack thereof. This passage is primarily concerned with the power of the Lord—the inevitable will of the One for whom all things are possible. Over the years, you will hear me say this again and again, if there is one lesson to be gleaned in all of scripture it is this: What God wants, God gets; God does as God wills, and this passage is no exception to this rule. And so, the Lord says to the prophet, *"Prophesy to these bones, and say to them: O dry bones, hear the word of the Lord. Thus, says the Lord God to these bones: I will cause breath to enter you, and you shall live. I will lay sinews on you, and will cause flesh to come upon you, and cover you with skin, and put breath in you, and you shall live; and you shall know that I am the Lord."*

Ezekiel does as he is instructed, and then we listen as the bones begin to rattle and shake, and in something reminiscent of a Hollywood science-fiction movie, we behold in awe and wonder as these dead and dry bones connect with one another to form skeletons. Sinews and tissue mystically coalesce from dust and air, gently wrapping bones and organs with muscle and skin as their former humanity begins to take shape before the prophet's eyes. However, the task is not yet complete. Although these old bones now have the appearance of life, they are not truly alive until the Lord commands his messenger to prophesy once again, so that the Spirit of the Lord may come upon the bodies from the four winds, filling their lungs with breath and restoring them to new life as members of God's beloved community.

And we hear the voice of the Lord again saying, *"And you shall know that I am the Lord, when I open your graves, and bring you up from your graves, O my people. I will put my spirit within you, and you shall live, and I will place you on your own soil; then you shall know that I, the Lord, have spoken and will act, says the Lord."*

Now we are Christians, of course, and almost every Sunday we stand up to affirm that part of the Apostles' Creed which states, "*I believe in the resurrection of the body*." That gets drilled into our heads after a while and so we assume that this vision foretells of our promised resurrection at the end of days. And certainly, the resurrection to new life is an important part of this message, but at the same time, that's not quite all there is. If we casually fall back into that mindset that this passage is about us and how God's promises will affect us personally, then we've missed an important part of the overall lesson. This passage is not just about our personal resurrection, it is about the hope and forgiveness that is present in the restoration of community. It is a community which (despite outward appearances) God has not abandoned—a community to which God has promised to remain faithful, even if it means going to unimaginable lengths to accomplish the impossible.

The prophet Ezekiel bears witness to a God who is present and at work among God's people, even throughout those times when God may appear absent. The story teaches us that wherever the Lord is, life and hope are made abundant and real. Of equal importance to our story is precisely *how* God is at work throughout the community of the faithful. For one, this restoration of which Ezekiel witnesses only comes about because of patiently listening for the Word of the Lord. And this doesn't happen quickly in a time and manner of our choosing. It comes about over time in a methodical and deliberate process as hand and eye slowly become knitted along with head and feet into an interconnected framework, forming the body once again by gradually bringing different parts together in unity with the whole, (and certainly not by splitting members apart). Yet even while possessing the physical form of a body, we remain just a shell of our former selves. Full restoration requires the presence of God's Spirit within us and among us so that we might once again live and love as God's chosen people.

Perhaps this congregation and perhaps the church might glean a lesson or two from the prophet. After all, we live in cynical times. In recent decades, we have seen as people and families in this nation have abandoned the church in droves, believing that the church has little to offer. We have seen the unity of Christ's church ripped apart by hubris and schism, fear and uncertainty. We have witnessed the church weakened, stripped down to little more than the skeletal remains of its former glory. And at times like these, we find ourselves wondering that very same question, "Can these bones live?" We have faith, sure…but the reality which surrounds us offers little consolation. Our eyes see nothing more than devastation and despair in a parched desert of hopelessness. Therefore, it can become all too easy to give up hope and simply assume our place among those lifeless bones. Yet we must remember…we have to struggle hard to remember that WE are the disciples of Jesus Christ. Even though to the world the church may by all outward measures appear to be dying, in the end, we do not believe in death; we believe in resurrection! We believe in restoration. We believe in reconciliation. And why? Not just because of what we have been promised, but because of what we have already received! Through Jesus Christ we have entered a new life of forgiveness and grace and in Jesus Christ we continue to experience that new life every moment of every day.

This is a message that the world needs to hear. The Lord needs warm bodies to declare the Word of the Lord to the world, rousing us from our slumber, bringing life to the lifeless, and proclaiming grace and forgiveness to those who see nothing but despair. The Lord needs those who possess the courage to reach out to those different from themselves, making real connections and further strengthening the body of faith. The Lord needs those who leave themselves open to the life-giving waters of the Spirit, that we may be enlivened and animated to do the difficult work of discipleship. The Lord needs those who possess perseverance to wait patiently for the restoration of hope, as well as the steadfastness and character to be that hope for someone else. The Lord needs those who are willing to be transformed and reformed into the very instruments of God's will. And by the time all is said and done, we may not even recognize ourselves, but we may rest assured that the God who calls us each by name has marked us as God's own.

Who are we? What are we doing here? To what purpose have we been raised? These are just some of the questions we will be asking ourselves as we begin this new journey together. Now all that remains is to take that next step, for it is the love of Christ that urges us on. And as we face the challenges of living as God's community of faith for our time and age, let us move assume this journey with confidence, remembering what God has done and what God is doing for God's people. For no matter what obstacles, we encounter, we know that God has already overcome greater things for our sake. So, united by our trust in God and guided by Word and Spirit we strive ever forward in our quest to become whole and complete people, as both individuals and as members of a common body of faith, while all along the way, we sing praises to God, saying…

Blessing and glory and wisdom and thanksgiving and honor and power and might be to our God forever and ever. Amen.

Whenever "Year B" rolls around in the Revised Common Lectionary, you quickly discover how the Gospel of Mark is undoubtedly my favorite of the four gospel witnesses. In fact, I routinely affirm the gospel to be one of the great works in the history of literature! What a rare quality, even for modern writers, to be able to create an immersive experience which effectively forces the reader toward a moral crisis point, whereby we as the audience are obligated to respond. This narrative approach not only communicates much about Christ, it also reveals a lot about us as his disciples! I find the Gospel of Mark theologically rich, brutally honest and bold in its declaration of the Good News. (It's what any decent pastor should aspire to be!) Of interest is the Jesus of Mark, who possesses the full range of human emotions, and experiences the many frustrations associated with ministry—a Jesus who even appears to struggle mightily with his identity as the Messiah. The original ending of 16:8 brings to fruition the true genius of Mark, whereby we discover ourselves alone, face-to-face with the mystery of the empty tomb. After everyone else has fled and gone, who will have the courage to follow in the way of Jesus Christ? Let's find out! Last one to Galilee is a rotten egg!

A Tough Crowd
July 5, 2015

1 [Jesus] left that place and came to his home town, and his disciples followed him. ²On the Sabbath he began to teach in the synagogue, and many who heard him were astounded. They said, 'Where did this man get all this? What is this wisdom that has been given to him? What deeds of power are being done by his hands! ³Is not this the carpenter, the son of Mary and brother of James and Joses and Judas and Simon, and are not his sisters here with us?' And they took offence at him. ⁴Then Jesus said to them, 'Prophets are not without honor, except in their home town, and among their own kin, and in their own house.' ⁵And he could do no deed of power there, except that he laid his hands on a few sick people and cured them. ⁶And he was amazed at their unbelief.

Then he went about among the villages teaching. ⁷He called the twelve and began to send them out two by two, and gave them authority over the unclean spirits. ⁸He ordered them to take nothing for their journey except a staff; no bread, no bag, no money in their belts; ⁹but to wear sandals and not to put on two tunics. ¹⁰He said to them, 'Wherever you enter a house, stay there until you leave the place. ¹¹If any place will not welcome you and they refuse to hear you, as you leave, shake *off the dust that is on your feet as a testimony against them.' ¹²So they went out and proclaimed that all should repent. ¹³They cast out many demons, and anointed with oil many who were sick and cured them.*

Mark 6:1-13 (NRSV)

As the famous early-20th century author Thomas Wolfe once observed, "You can't go home again." And based upon our scripture lesson, this proverb would appear to hold true, even for Jesus himself. As the sixth chapter of the Gospel of Mark gets underway, Jesus and his disciples have just arrived in his home town of Nazareth, after spending time ministering and preaching in nearby Galilee. Now, to set the scene, we have to recall all that has happened up to this point in the story. After being baptized in the Jordan by John and bearing witness to the Spirit descending upon him, Jesus calls his first disciples and begins teaching and performing great acts of power among the people. We follow them along as Jesus casts out many demons and heals others of various physical afflictions; paralysis, disfiguration, hemorrhages, just to name a few. We bear witness as Jesus stills a sudden storm, displaying mastery over all forms of human suffering, whether they be natural or supernatural in origin, or a byproduct of our mortal fears. Just the chapter before, Jesus even rescues a little girl from death itself!

And as Jesus and his disciples make their way through Galilee, his fame continues to increase to the extent that crowds of people are literally pressing in on him wherever he goes. All the while, Jesus and his disciples are constantly in motion. Mark is always telling us how, "Then he went here" and, "then they went there" and, "then they went back over here." Their pace is frenetic and exhausting. And wherever Jesus goes, his presence causes such a sensation that it proves nearly impossible for him to have even a moment of rest. Everywhere he turns there are people afflicted by this or that or something else. There is always someone just around the corner crying out to him for help. Jesus constantly finds himself awash in a sea of human misery from which there appears to be no end in sight.

Unlike the other three gospels, the Jesus portrayed in the gospel of Mark, is by far the most human. The gospels of Matthew and Luke leave no doubt as to Jesus' divine heritage, tracing his ancestry back through a distinguished line of patriarchs, prophets and kings, making it abundantly clear to the reader that Jesus has been the Christ from his very birth. John takes matters even further, portraying Christ as the divine Word incarnate, existing before the very foundations of the world, God literally walking among us in full and complete control of all events which transpire around him.

The Jesus of Mark, however, is quite different. In Mark, Jesus' human side assumes center stage, as we the reader are left wondering, "Who is this man? Where did he come from?" Indeed, these are questions that even Jesus himself appears to be struggling with, perhaps being vaguely unsure of exactly who he is and to what purpose this mysterious Spirit has been leading him. We see instances in Mark where Jesus' divine power appears to ebb and flow; he frequently loses his temper, sometimes lashing out at those around him. Still, there are other times in Mark's gospel where Jesus appears to be uncertain of whether he even *wants* to be the Christ, and therefore, as this journey takes him ever so closer to the cross, we as the audience are left in suspense, asking ourselves, "Will he, or won't he?" "Could he, or, even *should* he?"

Therefore, when Jesus suddenly turns up at his home town of Nazareth one day, we are unsure as to the exact purposes of his visit. It makes us wonder: What was he seeking? What did Jesus hope to find along those familiar streets and avenues? Was he seeking comfort and rest, was he seeking validation or recognition? Was he seeking escape or avoidance of his divine obligation? Was he seeking to reconnect in some way with his humanity, his family or his heritage?
Whatever Jesus came to Nazareth looking for, it quickly becomes apparent that he will be unable find it. We already know from Mark how Jesus' fame has spread across the region, throughout Galilee and the Decapolis and far beyond. He has already accomplished so many great and wonderful things, and yet when Jesus arrives home, he receives a rather frosty reception.

"*Where did this man get all this?*" the people cry sarcastically as Jesus begins to preach. "*What is this wisdom…? What deeds of power are being done by his hands! Is not this the carpenter, the son of Mary…are not his brothers and sisters here with us?*" And Mark notes how the people of Nazareth took *offense* at him; they cannot even offer Jesus the courtesy of referring to him by name. Instead, Jesus becomes disparagingly reduced to, "that guy", not a respected teacher, but, "the *carpenter*", not a fully-formed adult, but "the *son of Mary*." We soon recognize that, to go where God was calling him, Jesus had to give up his former, comfortable and predictable life as a tradesman back in his home town.

Now today, if someone wants to work in an occupation different from what their parents did for a living, it's okay; it's even encouraged at times. We wouldn't think anything of it, but in Jesus' day, such an idea was scandalous! The son was *expected* to follow his father in the family trade, as was his son, and so on and so on. To reject one's trade was tantamount to rejecting one's family, and to reject one's family was to reject the entire community in which that person was raised. So, in Nazareth, it is deliberately pointed out to Jesus that he is essentially *persona non-grata*, an unwelcome man without a home. And why? Because he had the audacity to leave while all his sisters and brothers did what was acceptable and stayed put. (Moreover, he even went as far as to dismiss that very same family chapters earlier when they attempted to corral him and bring him back to Nazareth!)

In our Christian experience, so much emphasis is placed upon a Christ who understands our fears and our concerns and can sympathize with us in our time of need. Very rarely do we find instances in the gospels where those tables become turned, and we discover ourselves to be the ones sympathizing with Jesus, especially during those moments when the fullness of his humanity becomes glaringly apparent. This episode in Nazareth is certainly one to which almost any pastor can relate. I've had the experience of going back to my home church to preach before, and whereas I can confidently say that I fared *far* better than Jesus did, it's still a humbling experience. Even though that church supported me with their prayers and gifts and encouragement throughout my time in seminary, there will always be that voice inside of my head that will wonder how seriously these people can take me as a pastor, teacher and leader in the church.

It's as if I can almost hear them saying, "Is this not the *starving artist*, the son of Mary and
George, Jr.? Is this not the boy who would cut up during worship, or leave the window to the Sunday school room unlocked so he and his friends could sneak in to play basketball in the gym? Is this not the child who raided the kitchen refrigerator to eat all our chicken salad? (Which, for the record, I *never* did!) Is this not the teenager who would climb the roof of the education building to lob water balloons upon his unsuspecting classmates? (Which I *may* have done…) Is this not the man who fled to seminary in Virginia because he couldn't make an honest living any other way?" Now, I love my home church, just as I love all the people who walk through its doors, but at the same time, I am humbled by the fact that it really doesn't matter how wonderful my sermon may be, or what I may accomplish professionally, I know that I have already provided the home crowd with every excuse they

will ever need *not* to listen to what I must say. I have come to understand what Jesus means when he says that, *"Prophets are not without honor, except in their home town."* I mean, it's nice to visit the folks back home, but when all is said and done, I understand that there's only so much good I can do there.
It's obvious my call and my vocation lie elsewhere.

And so, returning to our scripture lesson, Mark's gospel then remarks that Jesus, *"could do no deed of power [in Nazareth], except that he laid his hands on a few sick people and cured them."* Mark then goes on to say how, *"he was amazed…amazed…at their unbelief."* Mark's gospel is also unique in the way that there appears to be a very close relationship between people's faith and Jesus' ability to perform miracles. There are instances in the gospel where Jesus is able perform miracles even from considerable distances due to the greatness of a person's faith [7:29]. And as he will later tell the father of a boy suffering from violent seizures,
"All things can be done for the one who believes." [9:23] But based upon Jesus' experience in Nazareth, the opposite would also appear to be true, as even Jesus himself is unable to accomplish very much due to the community's lack of faith.

Stories such as these invite us to ask serious questions regarding the nature of faith versus the nature of doubt. As Christians, we tend to view faith and doubt as opposites, that faith somehow begins where doubt ends and vice versa. But we are all people of faith, and yet at the same time, we all have our doubts, so perhaps we need to reconsider this mindset. When we say "doubt", to what exactly are we referring? Is doubt expressed a genuine, intellectual exploration of the rational, known universe, or is doubt something altogether different? Would Mark even consider, "doubt" and, "unbelief" the same thing? What Mark considers unbelief appears to be manifested, not in doubt, but in the Nazarenes' cynicism and antipathy toward Jesus—their unwillingness to listen or entertain possibilities which come from life in true fellowship with the Lord. Faith, by extension, is not manifest in some false piety or moral superiority, but comes about by means of a genuine openness—a vulnerability if you will—which stems from a desperate yearning for Christ's presence and the Good News which he brings. Miracles, after all, are intended to teach us something about who our Lord is, but if we stubbornly believe that we have nothing to learn, then we close ourselves off to the presence of the Spirit among us. No progress will ever be possible by endeavoring to remain the same!

Perhaps in that sense, Jesus' next words to his disciples are no mystery as he instructs them to go forth into the world to teach the Good News. He tells them that to do this, they are going to have to get out of their comfort zone. They are going to have to travel light, letting go of material possessions and taking with them only the barest of essentials. They will have to leave everything that is safe and familiar behind so that they could be free to journey to faraway and unexpected places. They will have to transcend social and cultural barriers to seek out the lost and to lay their hands upon those who society and religion deem unclean, all while placing their welfare wholly in the hands of strangers. Jesus concedes to his disciples that not everyone will listen to this message of repentance and forgiveness from sin, *but the right ones will,* for there will be always someone out there who needs to hear the life-giving and sustaining promises of our Lord.

But as human beings, this is not how we are wired. We instinctively seek comfort, safety and stability among the customary and familiar, and so we insulate ourselves with people who look like we do and who act as we do and who share our beliefs and values. We wrap ourselves in symbols and emblems that declare to the world, "This is *who* I am, this is *where* I come from and this is *what* I believe," and we are unapologetic…*unapologetic*…in our defense of them. We refuse to give an inch! Anyone different, we regard with suspicion. Anyone who disagrees, we assume the problem to be with them, not with us. Anyone who criticizes, we take such matters as a personal affront to our character. Openness is regarded as liability, and vulnerability as weakness! The very foundation of our identity becomes so wrapped up in these external trappings, that after a while, we forget who we are and what we have been charged to do. Now, it's a good thing to honor and celebrate things greater than ourselves, but at what point does the gravitational pull of "tradition" and "values" hold us back and hinder us from putting ourselves out there to love and serve our Lord?

Perhaps upon those streets of Nazareth so very long ago, fate (or perhaps divine providence) had a very valuable lesson to teach Jesus' disciples about the true nature of Christian mission: With Jesus Christ, there is simply no going back. There is no settling down nor any safe hideaway in which to take comfort. There is no refuge from where we can insulate ourselves from the many problems facing the world. As disciples, our commission is as it always has been, to get *out there* to make a difference. The journey of the Good News is one which always looks forward, never behind. We have been granted authority to make our way to the next place, to the next town to the next challenge—to make our way just a little further down the road to get to where we are needed. And I'll be quite honest, given the many problems of this world, given the sheer scale and magnitude of human suffering that lays before us, it's so, so easy to lose heart. We see an endless parade of broken people, broken communities, broken relationships, and no doubt we think to ourselves, "This is going to take a miracle."

But for the body of Jesus Christ, such miracles are truly possible for those who believe. Reconciliation is possible. Transformation is possible. Renewal is possible. Forgiveness and healing are possible. All it takes is just a little faith!

Blessing and glory and wisdom and thanksgiving and honor and power and might be to our God forever and ever. Amen.

No compilation of Presbyterian sermons would be complete without at least one about predestination. This may be the most misunderstood of all Presbyterian beliefs, because...well...it's not Presbyterian at all! Predestination has always been a fundamental element of Judeo-Christian theology since the very beginning! So, when we speak of predestination, of what exactly are we speaking? Critics of predestination will claim it to be at odds with human free will, but the two are theological apples and oranges. At its heart, predestination merely expresses trust in the sovereignty of God. It is the belief that, whether human beings act in accordance God's will, or in opposition, God's intentions for creation will come to their inevitable completion. Nevertheless, our dependence upon God may be the most difficult thing for us to accept, especially for those living in a society which idolizes personal independence and the myth of the "self-made man". No matter where I have served as a pastor, congregation members frequently inquire about predestination, as it seems to raise more questions than answers. But then again, "answers" are not really the point, are they? No doctrine of predestination can ever be perfect, because our understanding of the mystery of God's will can never be perfect. It seems to change depending on time and circumstance. But regardless of what challenges the Christian community faces, it is vital to express our trust and faith in the divine providence of God's sovereign love!

Pick of the Litter

3 Blessed be the God and Father of our Lord Jesus Christ, who has blessed us in Christ with every spiritual blessing in the heavenly places, ⁴just as he chose us in Christ before the foundation of the world to be holy and blameless before him in love. ⁵He destined us for adoption as his children through Jesus Christ, according to the good pleasure of his will, ⁶to the praise of his glorious grace that he freely bestowed on us in the Beloved. ⁷In him we have redemption through his blood, the forgiveness of our trespasses, according to the riches of his grace ⁸that he lavished on us. With all wisdom and insight ⁹he has made known to us the mystery of his will, according to his good pleasure that he set forth in Christ, ¹⁰as a plan for the fullness of time, to gather up all things in him, things in heaven and things on earth. ¹¹In Christ we have also obtained an inheritance, having been destined according to the purpose of him who accomplishes all things according to his counsel and will, ¹²so that we, who were the first to set our hope on Christ, might live for the praise of his glory. ¹³In him you also, when you had heard the word of truth, the gospel of your salvation, and had believed in him, were marked with the seal of the promised Holy Spirit; ¹⁴this is the

> *pledge of our inheritance towards redemption as God's own people, to the praise of his glory.*   Ephesians 1:3-14(NRSV)

Predestination…perhaps you are familiar with this term. It appears to be one of those curious theological quirks that distinguishes the beliefs of Presbyterians from that of other Christian traditions. Sometimes, I'll find in conversation with a group of people and the topic will turn to what we do for a living. I'll mention that I am a Presbyterian pastor, and every now and again (not always, but often enough) someone will say to me, "Oh! You're Presbyterian! You believe in *predestination*, don't you?" And when I inevitably reply, "Yes", they look at me with some odd combination of wonder and befuddlement, as if they had just unearthed some curious relic from Christianity's ancient past.

But it's not like Presbyterians invented predestination. It's a theological idea that has been in existence in one form or another for millennia—long before the Protestant Reformation, before the Early Church Fathers, even before the Bible (as we know it) was even written. The truth is, almost all Christians affirm some belief in predestination (heck, even the pope believes in predestination) but admittedly, other traditions haven't placed the same emphasis upon it which ours historically has. I think it's safe to assume that virtually all Christians believe in a God who is all-knowing and all-powerful, that God knows the consequences of our actions for better or for worse. This is all pretty orthodox stuff which has changed very little over the course of the last two-thousand-plus years.

But what exactly is predestination? People often confuse predestination with fate, which is something completely different, or they mistakenly believe predestination to be the opposite of free will—that predestination implies that we have no real say in what we do—as if human beings are merely preprogrammed automatons operating according to the whim of some divine puppet-master. Yet nothing could be further from the truth. When we speak of human will and God's divine predestination, we are talking about two entirely different things. What it really comes down to is a difference in perception; whereas human perception of time and future is limited, God's is not. Moreover, predestination places confidence that there is a God who is present, active and at work throughout human history, so that God's ultimate plan for all creation will be carried out, *"in the fullness of time."*

I will easily confess that predestination is confusing and difficult to explain. Even our Presbyterian founding-father, John Calvin, would be the first to admit this. Calvin wrote, "*When they inquire into predestination, they are penetrating the sacred precincts of divine wisdom. If anyone with carefree assurance breaks into this place, he will not succeed in satisfying his curiosity and he will enter into a labyrinth from which he can find no exit.*"[1] Calvin became famous—or some might say, notorious—for a theological concept commonly described as, "Double Predestination", the idea that God has ordained from the beginning of time which people among us will be saved (the "Elect") and which will be condemned (the "Reprobate"). Or, to borrow words from the Gospel of Matthew, "Sheep over here, and goats over here!" Calvin believed that God raises up whom God chooses, God hardens the heart of whom God chooses, all so God may accomplish God's intentions for humanity and for creation.

Calvin was highly criticized for this teaching, even in his own lifetime, as many claimed that it portrayed God as unnecessarily cruel and uncaring. We do indeed believe in an all-powerful God, but at the same time, do we not also believe in a God who is all-merciful and all-forgiving as well? How can the idea of a loving and compassionate God be consistent with the idea of arbitrarily condemning people to damnation? And besides, how can one who is elect or saved rest comfortably in heaven with the knowledge that those they love may be languishing below in the hereafter?

All excellent questions…but it's just a theory, after all. No one ever said it was perfect. But understanding John Calvin's doctrine of double predestination also means understanding the time in which it originated. Calvin observed in his day how there were *grave* abuses within Western Christianity, as leaders in the Roman Catholic Church sought to establish themselves as the sole arbitrators in matters of human salvation. They claimed that those who did good works on behalf of the church would be rewarded in the next life, while those who spoke out against the authority of the church would be punished accordingly. By emphasizing predestination, John Calvin sought to rescue the salvation of humankind from the institution of the church by reestablishing Christian trust and faith in nothing less than the *sovereignty of God*. In fact, all of John Calvin's theology, and indeed everything we believe as Presbyterians must be understood according to this singular principle.

But that's really our problem, isn't it? To place our trust in God—someone that we cannot see or touch or converse with—someone whose presence we only receive passing glimpses of at best? That's just not our way. We're human beings after all; we crave certainty above all else. We don't want to *trust* that we are saved, we want to *know* that we are saved! And we see how there are many denominations and pastors out there who sell the idea that we can easily choose the path to our salvation—that our ultimate destiny rests in our hands and our hands alone. No need to worry about the other guy; they're on their own! But you can save yourself your own personal seat in heaven by simply doing this, or by believing that. Now, that's easy! That's money in the bank! That's guaranteed my friend!

But unfortunately, we are Presbyterians; we do not deal in certainty, only faith. Guarantees are easy. I could stand up in the pulpit and guarantee you almost anything and I would probably do quite well for myself in my career as a pastor. But in all good conscience, the only thing I can ever truly assure you of is the steadfast and sure love of God. Maybe that should be enough for us, but as Christians, placing our trust in God's love is the hardest thing we will ever do. It's hard because of our nature; it's hard because of our fears; it's hard because of our pride. Still, you must ask yourself: Given a so-called "choice", who are you most comfortable with deciding *your* ultimate destiny? You, or God? Well speaking for myself, I think I'm going to have to go with God on this one, and I'm confident you might feel the same way.

So, in the grand scheme of things, exactly *how* we are predestined might be far less important than *what* we are predestined to. Perhaps predestination is less concerned with our individual circumstance, but instead is how he sovereign will of God is expressed through the community of the faithful, *"so that we, who were the first to set our hope on Christ, might live for the praise of his glory."* In that light, it becomes clear that the church was never intended by God as a place from which to judge others. It was never meant to be a refuge where self-important people decide who is in and who is out of the Kingdom of God. God instead created the church so that it might become the instrument of God's grace in the world, a gathering place where all people are welcome to experience God's love and forgiveness firsthand.

Therefore, when considering the mystery of God's will, we must remember our calling to *be* the church. *Going* to church is one thing, but *being* the church is something entirely different. To love one another, to care for one another, to be assume one another's fears and burdens through the sharing of our collective strength—that is what it means to live and act as the Body of Christ. We must be this radical, self-giving community of faith envisioned in the scriptures, where, the presence of the Holy Spirit among us marks us as God's own. This will not make us popular. This doesn't necessarily mean that young families with children are going to come flooding through the doors every Sunday morning, but this does involve keeping the doors open just in case they might. God does not demand moral perfection, nor does God require a flawless faith or pristine piety. God simply expects us to be the church, for when we are united with one another in true Spirit of love and fellowship, we are being the people who God created us to be.

When we look out into the world and the people who live in it, it can be as if we have just walked into an antique store where all we see is wall-to-wall junk. But the wisdom of God can discern how there is treasure hidden among these dusty shelves, and so God proves willing to pay whatever cost is necessary to take the whole lot. Now, some may be corroded by hatred or fear, while others may be rusted through due to apathy or neglect; clearly, there is much brokenness to be found. And yet, with the right amount of care, the hand of God can accomplish wonders beyond our imagining. Therefore, as God's community of faith, let us place ourselves in God's hands. Let us not worry over things that are beyond our control, but instead concern ourselves with what those things that lie firmly within our grasp: Helping one another, loving one another, reaching out to each other with that same grace and forgiveness by which we have been so richly and abundantly blessed.

God has destined God's people for good things, so let us receive our inheritance with joy!

Blessing and glory and wisdom and thanksgiving and honor and power and might be to our God forever and ever. Amen.

1. Calvin, John, *The Institutes of the Christian Religion, III.xxi.1*, ed. John T. McNeill, Westminster John Knox Press,
1960

Who are the Pharisees? Historically speaking, they one of many political and religious sects active in first-century Judaism. Many Christian tenets, like predestination, the resurrection of the dead and even, "The Priesthood of All Believers" have some origin within Pharisaic Judaism. Some scholars have even suggested that Jesus himself was a Pharisee, and that his conflict with them in the gospels is symptomatic of an internal conflict within a religious tradition. Regardless, when reading the gospels, the task for the exegete is to understand how the Pharisees function in a narrative context. What role do they play in the story? Aside from acting as a foil for the protagonist, the Pharisees embody religious attitudes which are unfortunately all too common, even today. The Pharisees view religion as a means of validating a privileged station in life. Faith becomes perverted into a means of excluding others from full participation in the life and fellowship of the community of faith, while ignoring their own need for divine grace. Jesus' ministry to the poor and marginalized exposes this hypocrisy, but rather than repent from self-serving ways, the Pharisees find it far easier to look for fault in Jesus, and Jesus' generous nature provides them with all they seek! But then again, perhaps the Pharisees might have gotten just a little more than they bargained for…

Beware to those brave enough to claim the moral high ground. It's a long way down!

Letter of the Law

1 Now when the Pharisees and some of the scribes who had come from Jerusalem gathered around him, ²they noticed that some of his disciples were eating with defiled hands, that is, without washing them.³ (For the Pharisees, and all the Jews, do not eat unless they thoroughly wash their hands, thus observing the tradition of the elders; ⁴and they do not eat anything from the market unless they wash it; and there are also many other traditions that they observe, the washing of cups, pots, and bronze kettles.) ⁵So the Pharisees and the scribes asked him, 'Why do your disciples not live according to the tradition of the elders, but eat with defiled hands?' ⁶He said to them, 'Isaiah prophesied rightly about you hypocrites, as it is written,

> *"This people honors me with their lips,*
> *but their hearts are far from me; ⁷ in*
> *vain do they worship me,*
> *teaching human precepts as doctrines."*

⁸You abandon the commandment of God and hold to human tradition.'

14 Then he called the crowd again and said to them, 'Listen to me, all of you, and understand: ¹⁵there is nothing outside a person that by going in can defile, but the things that come out are what defile.'

17 When he had left the crowd and entered the house, his disciples asked him about the parable. ¹⁸He said to them, 'Then do you also fail to understand? Do you not see that whatever goes into a person from outside cannot defile, ¹⁹since it enters, not the heart but the stomach, and goes out into the sewer?' (Thus, he declared all foods clean.) ²⁰And he said, 'It is what comes out of a person that defiles. ²¹For it is from within, from the human heart, that evil intentions come: fornication, theft, murder, ²²adultery, avarice, wickedness, deceit, licentiousness, envy, slander, pride, folly. ²³All these evil things come from within, and they defile a person.'

Mark 7:1-8, 14-23(NRSV)

I have no qualms declaring *The Gospel of Mark* to be my favorite among the four gospels. It is an intense, revealing, and sometimes intimate exploration of discipleship and the person of Jesus Christ. Very often the reader is brought into the story through situations which demand a response from Christ's followers. The question of "Who is Jesus Christ?" dominates the narrative, and it is a question to which we will not receive an answer until we reach that fateful cross on Calvary. Until then, however, everyone seems to have their own opinion regarding who Jesus is. Therefore, when someone approaches Jesus in Mark's gospel, you must wonder about their motives. What are they looking for? Why do they seek Christ? Suffice it to say, in this journey of life, what we are seeking reveals a lot about who we are!

As the seventh chapter opens in the Gospel of Mark, we see how Pharisees and scribes have "gathered around" Jesus as he teaches to the assembled crowds in Galilee. It is noted that some of them have traveled from as far as Jerusalem to see him in person, as Jesus' fame has traveled across the land in such a short period of time. Mark specifically identifies these people who are here to see Jesus, and so we have to wonder once again, "What are these people looking for? Why have these scribes and Pharisees come before Jesus this day?" And it does not take long for their motives to become revealed to the reader. What are they looking for? They are waiting for Jesus to make a mistake. We have already known since chapter three how the Pharisees have conspired with the Herodians to "destroy" Jesus, and so they come before him searching for anything they can use against Jesus to discredit him and to possibly have him arrested.

It turns out, it doesn't take them very long to find something. As they are watching closely, they notice how some of Jesus' disciples eat without ritually washing their hands first. Normally, washing your hands before eating is good thing and we want to encourage this, but we must bear in mind that this case has very little to do with cleanliness or sanitation. The act of washing one's hands was (as Mark notes) one of just many religious rituals that the ancient Jews observed. Sensing an opportunity, they publicly accuse Jesus,
"Why do **your** *disciples not live according to the tradition of the elders, but eat with defiled hands?"* They attempt to spring that classic fundamentalist trap. We hear such rhetoric in the religious absolutism of our own day, especially as it applies to scripture. "The Bible is either 100% right or it's 100% wrong!" they will cry. "A rejection of any part of it constitutes a rejection of all of it!" Confident in what scripture says, the Pharisees believe they have Jesus cornered, for if there is something wrong with the disciple, then it stands to reason that there must be something wrong with the teacher, and if there is something wrong with the teacher, then there must be something wrong with what that teacher teaches!

However, as he often does, Jesus quickly turns the tables on his critics saying, *"Isaiah prophesied rightly about you hypocrites, as it is written, 'This people honors me with their lips, / but their hearts are far from me; / in vain do they worship me, / teaching human precepts as doctrines.'"* He then accuses the accusers declaring, "**You** *abandon the commandment of God and hold to human tradition.*" It is, oddly enough, the exact same thing of which the Pharisees have accused Jesus. Yet in Jesus' view, it is not the disciples who have forsaken the law, but rather the Pharisees, who twist the Word of God into something it is NOT, that is, a litmus test that they may use to gauge the moral failings of others. They abuse the law, citing chapter and verse of "the rules" to advance their narrowminded agenda. Jesus makes it clear that such self-righteous nonsense only serves to defile the Word of God and the purposes for which God has sent it, just as their words and their actions seek to defile Christ himself (the divine Word incarnate) as well!

Now, we should be careful not to take matters to the other extreme by assuming that Jesus is telling his disciples to reject religious tradition altogether. (Presbyterians should be particularly sensitive to this.) Even Jesus understood the value within religious observance and ritual, as he himself was a devout Jew. Ultimately, fault is found in the Pharisees, not with the law. But Jesus does force us to consider the question, "What is the purpose of the law? Toward what end did God provide us the gift of scripture to begin with?" Are we seeking to advance a point-of-view, or are we using the Word as God intended, to glorify God and to accomplish God's will? Our motives matter. In many ways, the reasons *why* we do something is far, far more important what we do.

You will hear me say this again and again and again: *There is no greater heresy than to use the gift of holy scripture to win an argument.* Yet we see it all the time! A controversy erupts in the church over this or that or the other and people go running as quickly as they can to the pages of scripture. This side will pick this verse and this verse and this verse which supports their argument here and the other side will pick that verse and that verse and that verse which supports their argument there, and they'll go back and forth and back and forth; they will bicker and fight and accuse and defend. The complete witness of scripture is neglected, the historical circumstances which gave rise to scripture is forgotten altogether, the social and religious context of the words is wholly ignored, all so people can have the luxury of saying, "*I told you so!*" And this endless back and forth and back and forth accomplishes *nothing*, other than to wear away at the fabric of our Christian unity.

And people see these conflicts and constant moral judgments among the Christian community (which incidentally, should know better) and they are put off my religion. They hear the things we say and see how we behave amongst ourselves as evidences of our own hypocrisy, and so they are content to throw the proverbial baby out with the bathwater and reject religious belief altogether as something without value. They see the church as an irrelevant institution fixated on the past, taking the round peg of ancient religious "tradition" and attempting to force it through the square hole of modern, 21st century social issues. And guess what? *They are right!* Either we are God's faithful community, or we are not. Either we are Christ's disciples, or we are not. If it is not plainly obvious to *everyone*, then we only have ourselves to blame. So, we must ask ourselves: To what tradition do *we* belong? Is it one of pettiness and moral judgment, or is it one built upon generosity, forgiveness and love? Is it one of exclusivity and making distinctions among us, or is it one of inclusivity and welcome? Do the traditions of our past hold us prisoner, or do they *set us free* so that we may love and serve our Lord?

God wants us to be God's people now! God wants us to be God's servants now! God wants us to accept the challenge of living as Christ's disciples so that we may address the problems and injustices of our day and age. Scripture can offer us guidance in these matters. Scripture can offer us some insight into the human condition by reminding us where we stand in relation to God. If we see where the Holy Spirit was at work in the past, then perhaps we can see with greater clarity where the Spirit is working in the present. But if we reduce the gift of scripture down to a simple set of "Thou shalt nots…" then we have really missed the point. When people use scripture to make petty and superficial moral distinctions among us, or pervert it to alienate people from the community of faith, then people have forgotten the purposes for which that scripture was provided, that is, to underscore our collective brokenness and our mutual need for divine grace. Perhaps nowhere is that brokenness better evidenced than in our casual manipulation of the Word to suit our own ends.

"Listen to me, all of you, and understand," Jesus says. *"There is nothing outside a person that by going in can defile, but the things that come out are what defile…For it is from within, from the human heart, that evil intentions come."* Whereas the Pharisees are quick to make moral distinctions between themselves and Jesus' disciples, Jesus, by contrast, refuses to do so. "Listen to me, *ALL* of you," he declares to disciple and Pharisee alike. Regardless of whether we consider ourselves to be saint or sinner, relative to the Lord's greatness, we all fall woefully short. We are all so very different people and we spend so much time and energy trying to distinguish ourselves in this world, yet isn't it ironic to discover that really the only thing that we all share as human beings is the fact that, under the letter of the law, we all stand convicted! Strangely enough, this is where we find unity, not in our virtue, but in our guilt.

Yet we only magnify this culpability when otherwise good people passively acquiesce to forms of moral intimidation. Even when our friends or neighbors may say something which doesn't quite sit right with us, we rationalize and say to ourselves, "Oh, these are decent, Christian people…they wouldn't say it if it weren't true." And so, we silently go along with such judgments because we don't want to "rock the boat" as it were, nor do we wish to invite similar attention upon ourselves. But Jesus has the courage (and moreover the knowledge) to call out hypocrisy where he sees it. Try as we might, we cannot justify ourselves morally or ethically because of those things that emerge from our hearts—the hearts of *all people* not just those who struggle in this world. Scripture teaches us that only God can justify. Only God judges what is worthy and righteous. Only God determines who is welcomed into God's kingdom.

Should you spend your time constantly searching for fault in someone, then guess what? You'll be happy to know that you won't have to wait very long. Soon you will find *exactly* what you seek. (Hey, you can even use scripture to justify it!) But be warned! The things that you are seeking may end up revealing a lot more about you, than the person you so scrutinize. The Gospel of Mark begs the question, what are *you* looking for when you approach Jesus? If you will notice, those, "morally upright, decent and religious" people who seek to justify themselves before the Savior…well, they never fare so well. Yet regardless of whether it is in the form of a desperate foreign mother, a blind beggar by the roadside or countless others plagued by sickness or mental illness, the most faithful examples in scripture come before Jesus seeking healing, wholeness and forgiveness, because they *know*—they know such things are Christ's and Christ's alone to provide.

If we truly consider ourselves to be a faithful people, then we must acknowledge our own desperate need for Christ's help. Fortunately for us, Jesus routinely demonstrates how, despite our many faults, we have each been welcomed into a tradition of grace and love. If we can set aside the folly of moral judgment, we might make just enough room in our hearts so that God can fill us with good things!

Blessing and glory and wisdom and thanksgiving and honor and power and might be to our God forever and ever. Amen.

As I mentioned before, I belong to a congregation which understands brokenness. The scars of having been a church in conflict have faded, yet are still visible in many ways. The saddest part is that most of it could have been avoided with just a little compassion and understanding. When I have spoken with other churches undergoing similar conflict, I discover that it is usually driven by a small, vocal minority who claim to speak for the congregation when most simply want the fighting to cease. Many self-righteous pastors and leaders routinely fail to understand that it is not dogma or theology which drive people away from the church, it is the conflict itself. The supreme crisis in church and society today is not one of piety, but one of moral absolutism, where people cannot accept those who may disagree with them on a variety of social, religious or political issues. If one uses Christian faith to validate one's beliefs, rather than challenge them, I would have deep concerns about their sincerity. Disagreement has always been part of the Christian experience—always has, always will. When all we can see is conflict, the challenge for the faithful is how to regain our focus, to keep mission and true righteousness at the center of community.

Forced Perspectives

30 They went on from there and passed through Galilee. He did not want anyone to know it; ³¹for he was teaching his disciples, saying to them, 'The Son of Man is to be betrayed into human hands, and they will kill him, and three days after being killed, he will rise again.' ³²But they did not understand what he was saying and were afraid to ask him.

33 Then they came to Capernaum; and when he was in the house he asked them, 'What were you arguing about on the way?' ³⁴But they were silent, for on the way they had argued with one another about who was the greatest. ³⁵He sat down, called the twelve, and said to them, 'Whoever wants to be first must be last of all and servant of all.' ³⁶Then he took a little child and put it among them; and taking it in his arms, he said to them, ³⁷'Whoever welcomes one such child in my name welcomes me, and whoever welcomes me welcomes not me but the one who sent me.'

Mark 9:30-37 (N█V)

Every now and again I will find myself talking with a friend or a colleague about the present state of the church in the world, and inevitably, all the recent divisions within our Presbyterian denomination will enter the conversation. We will converse about recent debates over ordination and marriage and the PC(USA)'s response to a variety of controversial issues in our nation and in the world, from Israel-Palestine, to immigration, to gun control and everything in between. And occasionally, someone will roll their eyes up toward the heavens and say something like this: "[Sigh] You know, I wish the church could go back to the way it was in the beginning, without all the divisions, disagreements and discord, when the church one and was focused on its mission in the world." It's such a lovely thought, but being the notorious cynic that I am, I always reply, "A church without division? A church without disagreement? Wow…What Bible have YOU been reading?"

Many good and faithful people often wax romantically about this church of the ancient past, where everyone got along with one another, where the church's mission in the world was clear, where truth and understanding were in fruitful abundance, but I however, am placed in the unfortunate position of having to remind people, this church of which we so nostalgically dream simply *never existed*. Now of course, there is the early church as it is portrayed in the Book of Acts, where the early apostles shared equally in their possessions and distributed them all, *"as any had need"* [2:45, 4:35], where Christians were of one mind in terms of ministry and mission to spread the Good News of Jesus Christ out into the far reaches of the known world. The Book of Acts paints a beautiful and marvelous portrait of the cooperative, communal nature of the early church, and it is also one which is completely contradicted by scripture itself!

If you read the letters of Paul, then you receive a very different depiction of the early church. In Galatians, Paul recounts an episode where he personally rebuked Peter to his face at Antioch for Peter's reluctance to share in fellowship with Gentile converts [Gal. 2:11-13]. And when you think about it, that's really the whole reason Paul wrote his letters in the first place, as they were each addressed to Christian congregations (and individuals) who were experiencing some measure of conflict—deep divisions caused by varying interpretations of scripture, pressing social issues, relations with those of other faiths, morals and ethics, church versus state—you know, pretty much the exact same things Christians like to argue over today! Whereas the Book of Acts may present a beautiful, albeit slightly embellished, portrait of the early church, history is not necessarily the goal of the Book of Acts. Acts does not seek to describe the church as it truly was, so much as it hopes to describe the church as it should be. Like many faithful Christians today, the author of the Book of Acts also longed for a time when Christ's church would truly be one!

To further illustrate my point, if we venture back to the ninth chapter of the Gospel According to Mark, we find Jesus and his disciples returning to Galilee after a recent sojourn north to Caesarea Philippi. At some point during this journey, an argument breaks out among Jesus' disciples about which one of them is the greatest. You must bear in mind where we are in the story. This is just a chapter after Peter's bold confession of Christ as, the Messiah, and just a few lines after the divine glory of Jesus was revealed to a small group of disciples at the Transfiguration. After all that the disciples have seen up to this point, after all they have experienced, if ever there were any moment that the disciples could get their act together and be inspired to act as a single body of faith—if ever there was a chance to finally "get it", you would think that now would be the time!

And yet by the end of the chapter, here we are, pretty much back to square one, and we find the disciples (true to form) squabbling among themselves over petty and trivial concerns. Jesus, incidentally, overhears their arguing, and understandable reasons, he decides that he does not have the patience to deal with them at that moment. Instead Jesus patiently waits until they have arrived at their destination, and then he asks the twelve, *"What were you arguing about on the way?"* and the disciples remain silent because they are too ashamed to reply. A few moments ago, they had all kinds of things to say about how great they were, but strangely, now words seem to elude them. And while the disciples stare into space avoiding eye contact with their teacher, Jesus then very deliberately gathers the twelve around him. He needs their complete and undivided attention if he is going teach them this most important of lessons. "Listen up!" he declares. *"Whoever wants to be first must be last of all and servant of all."* Then to drive home his point, Jesus takes a little child and places the child among them. Then taking the child into his arms, he says to them, *"Whoever welcomes one such child in my name welcomes me, and whoever welcomes me welcomes not me but the one who sent me."*

The proximity of this child at the very center of this group of disciples is crucial to the lesson. Today, children occupy a special place among our national priorities, but back in Jesus' day, things were quite different. Children were valued insomuch as they would one day become adults to carry on the family line, but in and of themselves, children enjoyed very little standing in society. There were no charities providing for the needs of children, nor any organizations advocating on their behalf. Until they reached adulthood, children in the ancient world essentially existed in society as "non-persons". (Even Mark refuses to regard the child in our lesson as, "he" or, "her", but rather as an "it".) Children represented everything a person did not want to be in that harsh and unforgiving world: weak, vulnerable and wholly dependent upon someone else, not just for their well being, but for their very identity.

By placing this child before them, it is as if Jesus is saying to his disciples, "If you truly consider yourself to be my followers, then this is who you are called to serve—the most vulnerable and powerless among us. If you want to be deemed worthy in the eyes of the Lord, then you must use the strength you possess to lift those in need—to reach out in compassion and concern, welcoming in the midst of you the sick, the lonely, the addicted, the oppressed, the suffering, the different—all of those 'non-persons' in the world which society so casually casts aside out of ignorance, selfishness, complacency or fear. If you are to be my disciples, it is not enough to simply sit around and hope for the best, you must be that hope to a world in need." During just three simple verses, Jesus completely reverses our popular understanding of what greatness truly entails.

In our Bible study on the Book of Genesis last Wednesday, we spent the hour discussing the creation story, and the many and wonderful ways God speaks to creation and through creation to accomplish God's intentions. After all, repeated words in scripture are very important, and when they come up again and again during a passage or story, they deserve special attention. At various times throughout the creation narrative, God utters the phrase, "*Let there be…*" and it immediately is the lesson being, what God wants, God gets. But it must be noted that when God says, "*Let there be light…*" God does not demand that the light be anything other than what it was created to be. God does not expect the light to be the wind any more than God expects a cow to be a bird. God has ordered the world in such a way that all its magnificent and diverse splendor might serve as a living testimony to God's greatness and graciousness.

"Let there be…" This is an important phrase to consider in our own lives of discipleship. I recently had lunch with Ben Brown, the new Associate Pastor for Youth at First Baptist, and he was lamenting the difficult time he has convincing parishioners to simply "be". And I can understand his frustration; people are not good at simply "being". We almost exclusively define ourselves, not by who we are, but by what we do. "Hey, what do you do?" "Well, I'm a pastor…I'm an attorney…I'm a teacher…I'm an engineer." We seek to establish our identity within our community by knowing all the right people and doing the right things to earn the approval and respect of our peers. We sacrifice life and labor, energy and emotion to justify ourselves in the eyes of others. We aspire to be known as the richest, the smartest, the toughest, the most popular, the most creative, or the most pious. In other words, we want to be the *greatest*. And to satisfy this ambition, we create all sorts of expectations for ourselves and others to live up to, and we judge all things, and all people, accordingly.

Yet all the while, God does not expect anything more from us other than what we were created to be, that is, blessed and beloved child of God, formed in God's very image. And just as God is gracious and loving to us, so are we to be to one another. Even throughout those times when we fall short, when we find ourselves at our most vulnerable, when we experience hardship or weakness or powerlessness, when it seems as if no one else in the world even cares about us, it is the hand of the Lord which lifts us up to embrace us among the company of Christ's disciples to remind us once again of who we are, and who we must endeavor to *be*. Perhaps accordingly, for our own sake, we need to allow Jesus to be who he was sent to be: our Teacher, our Redeemer, our Strength and our Counsel.

That is why I am constantly reminding you, that of all the things we as a body of faith can accomplish, the most important among these is to simply "be" the church. The church, after all, is who God has created us to be. Of course, we are far from perfect. Of course, we are fickle. Of course, we are flawed. Of course, we disagree, we bicker and argue. Of course, we can be shallow and self-serving at times. We demonstrate every day how the church is a very human institution complete with human limitations, and yet even so, God is still able to do wondrous things through us when we gather at our Lord's command, keeping Christ and the most vulnerable among us at the center of our ministry and mission. We can still be great; we just need someone to teach us how! Like us, God shows little interest in venturing to places where God is not welcome, therefore we must remain ever watchful when such opportunities present themselves. For if we know how Christ is present with the very least of these, embracing the needy and vulnerable, then perhaps our community of faith needs to recognize our dependence on the Lord so we may be counted among them as well.

Please do not be misled into assuming this vision of unified and holy church boldly proclaiming the Good News to the world to be some elusive, naïve pipe dream. Quite the contrary, it is a good and noble end to which we as a body of faith should always aspire! But as Jesus reminds his disciples, Christian unity is not discovered in dogma or theology nor experienced through conformity. Christian unity is only found in the cross—that sign of shared brokenness and a reminder how we have each been blessed by God's abundant grace. In Mark's Gospel, no one truly recognizes Jesus for who he is until his crucifixion. After all that we have seen and heard, *that* is the moment when we as Christ's disciples finally, "get it". The cross provides the focus for our mission in the world, informing us that the salvation of humankind was not purchased through a moment of power or so-called, "greatness", but rather it came about in a moment of sublime vulnerability the ultimate act of self-giving and humility which invites each of God's children to bear witness the tremendous lengths which God is willing to go to show God's great love for us.

Whenever our adventure as Christ's disciples finally reaches its conclusion, I'm curious to know whether we too will find our teacher at the end of our journey ready to pose us that very same question, "What were you arguing about on the way?" Like a true disciple, did you raise your voice in protest all the many injustices of this world, or did you simply join along in the idle chatter of lesser men? Did your words speak encouragement to the downtrodden, proclaim hope for the oppressed, or offer comfort for the grieving? I wonder if by the end of that journey we too will be rightly shamed, or will we be blessed with confident knowledge of the many ways we have already welcomed Christ into our midst? I suppose only time will tell…

Blessing and glory and wisdom and thanksgiving and honor and power and might be to our God forever and ever. Amen.

Like many rural communities, the Shenandoah Valley possesses a gun culture. Law abiding citizens own and use firearms every day to hunt, to hone their shooting skills, and even (on rare occasion) protect their homes and families. However, something is obviously broken in our society when military-grade handguns and assault rifles are made easily accessible to the mentally or emotionally disturbed, or misguided persons filled with hate. The most ironic thing is, that most of these gun owners (who organizations like the National Rifle Association claim to speak for) support tighter regulation on such weapons! No one has more of a vested interest in the responsible, legal ownership of guns than gun owners themselves. In the debate over gun control and gun access, I wholeheartedly believe common ground exists, therefore, there is little excuse for complacency by our elected leaders.

This is yet another sermon delivered in the wake of a, "Mass Shooting Event" (although "slaughter" or "massacre" would be far more appropriate). The fact we must keep inventing such anesthetized language should be sobering enough. This time, as with every time, I naively hoped it will be my last such message, but San Bernardino, Charleston, Orlando and many others would soon follow suit.

Lord, have mercy.

Place Your Bets

__1__ There was once a man in the land of Uz whose name was Job. That man was blameless and upright, one who feared God and turned away from evil.

__2__ One day the heavenly beings came to present themselves before the Lord, and Satan also came among them to present himself before the Lord. ²The Lord said to Satan, 'Where have you come from?' Satan answered the Lord, 'From going to and fro on the earth, and from walking up and down on it.' ³The Lord said to Satan, 'Have you considered my servant Job? There is no one like him on the earth, a blameless and upright man who fears God and turns away from evil. He still persists in his integrity, although you incited me against him, to destroy him for no reason.' ⁴Then Satan answered the Lord, 'Skin for skin! All that people have they will give to save their lives. ⁵But stretch out your hand now and touch his bone and his flesh, and he will curse you to your face.' ⁶The Lord said to Satan, 'Very well, he is in your power; only spare his life.'

> *7 So Satan went out from the presence of the Lord, and inflicted loathsome sores on Job from the sole of his foot to the crown of his head.⁸Job took a potsherd with which to scrape himself, and sat among the ashes.*
>
> *9 Then his wife said to him, 'Do you still persist in your integrity? Curse God, and die.' ¹⁰But he said to her, 'You speak as any foolish woman would speak. Shall we receive the good at the hand of God, and not receive the bad?' In all this Job did not sin with his lips.*
>
> Job 1:1, 2:1-10 (NRSV)

What are we supposed to do with the Book of Job? Of all the books in the bible, Job perhaps presents us with the greatest theological challenge. How can we place trust in an all-powerful, loving and compassionate God considering unjust human suffering? The problem of the suffering of the innocent: Admittedly, this is the "Achilles Heel" of the Christian faith, and one that no theologian from Augustine to Calvin to Niebuhr to Barth has ever been able to provide a satisfactory answer. As we attempt to faithfully navigate the religious landscape of the Book of Job searching for answers which will satisfy our need for comfort and justice, we instead find ourselves spinning our wheels upon the slippery surface of exasperation.

When the Book of Job opens, we find the heavenly host filing into the throne-room before the Lord, prepared to present themselves. Much to our surprise, we find Satan among them as well! Now, at this point, we must pause for a moment to appreciate Job as a story, to understand how the character of Satan functions in the narrative. In the Old Testament, Satan is not the personification of evil that later generations would make him out to be. In the Book of Job, Satan is acting as an *agent provocateur* of sorts, that is, it is his job is to test the loyalty of God's subjects by using a variety of means at his disposal. The scene that takes place before us in Job is not one where Satan and God are locked in some eternal struggle for the souls of humankind, no…Satan, like all the others, assumes his place among the heavenly host and prepares to make his report to the Lord.[1]

"Where have you come from?" the Lord asks Satan. Satan answers, "*From going to and fro on the earth, and from walking up and down on it.*" Per usual, Satan is expecting to tell God of all the disloyal people which he encountered along his way, all those high-minded, religious folks who would easily sell their integrity for the most astonishing of incentives. Yet before Satan can even get another word out of his mouth, the Lord interrupts, "*Have you considered my servant Job? There is no one like him on the earth, a blameless and upright man who fears God and turns away from evil.*" And Satan sarcastically replies, "Does Job fear God for nothing? Of course, he loves you…Look at all you have blessed Job with, family, wealth, abundance and good health. I'll bet you, that if you take all those things away from him, he will be just like every other person in the world and will curse your very name!"

With this declaration, Satan essentially makes a wager with God that this allegedly, "blameless and upright man" will prove just as easy to corrupt as any other human being. Corruption, after all, is something that Satan knows a great deal about. The wager is disturbing enough in and of itself, that there might be someone out there with a vested interest in our moral failings, but what makes matters even more unsettling is that God takes him up on his bet! "Very well, he is in your power," concedes the Lord. "Only spare his life." And so, Satan begins a deliberate process of bringing Job to ruination. First, bands of marauders come upon Job's herds and flocks, killing his servants and stealing his livestock. Job's children are killed after their home collapses in a violent windstorm. Satan causes boils to form upon Job's skin, and with everything (health, wealth and happiness) now taken away from him, Job sits among the broken pottery shards and darkened ashes of his former life, and yet still, Job refuses to curse God's name.

Now at this point in the story, you might think this means that God has officially won the bet. You might think that God, once having proved Job to be a blameless and faithful servant would now begin the process of restoring Job to some semblance of his former standing by rewarding him for this courageous display of faith. Yet strangely, there is nothing of the sort! You must bear in mind that this is literally just the beginning of the story; we're only at the beginning of chapter two! We have another forty grueling chapters of adversity and agony to muddle through before we arrive at any form of conclusion. And over the course of that time, Job's humiliation and lamentation will raise no shortage of uncomfortable questions for the faithful about what it means to place our trust in God who can at times appear to be absent or unconcerned about human suffering!

In his commentary *On Job: God-Talk and the Suffering of the Innocent*, a Roman Catholic theologian by the name of Gustavo Gutiérrez asserts that the Book of Job challenges the faithful with the question, "Can there ever be such a thing as a 'disinterested religion'"? That is, are human beings capable of retaining religious faith without resorting to some system of divine rewards and punishments? You see, in Satan's view, religious faith is merely pragmatic; it is simply a means to an end. He believes human beings only worship God because they seek some form of compensation in this life or the next either through good fortune or eternal salvation. But example of Job's faithfulness refutes Satan's cynicism, asserting that to maintain one's faith in the midst of suffering may, in the end, be faith's only true form. As Gutiérrez writes, "In self-seeking religion, there is no true encounter with God…"[2] Once suffering has stripped faith of all its external trappings and incentives, all that remains is trust. And this trust—this complete and undiluted dependence upon God—this assurance of God's presence and gratitude for God's mercy—is really the only relationship human beings can genuinely share with their Lord.

I think about this, especially in times when we once again come face-to-face with the suffering of the innocent, the latest glaring example taking place at a community college in Roseburg, Oregon (incidentally, a city almost identical in size, demographics and geography to our own community). As you may know already, nine people were killed in the shooting, and another nine people seriously wounded. And in the time since, we have put faces and names with the victims: students pursuing their dreams, a young parent preparing for a new career, a retiree seeking personal improvement through learning, a former addict trying to turn their life around, a teacher seeking to impart wisdom—all those hopes shattered because once again, some deluded sociopath in our nation managed to get his hands around a gun.

Now I will confess that my personal views on guns, gun safety and gun control are continually evolving. I'm philosophically against the creation of laws designed to curtail the rights of Americans out of the fear that someone *might* do something harmful. I understand the reasoning behind the inclusion of the Second Amendment to the United States Constitution. I understand that often many of the guns used in mass-shootings are obtained illegally or by circumventing existing gun laws. I understand that any conversation regarding gun control in our nation will be fruitless unless we address other contributing social factors including the lack of access to mental health care and our failed drug war. I understand that millions of law-abiding citizens responsibly own and use firearms every day without incident. I understand…I get all that. And yet time and time again I witness the sheer exasperation and frustration upon the faces of our nation's people and leaders who can offer nothing more than, "thoughts and prayers" to shattered and grieving communities.

It was the spring of 2007 when I first brought the reality of gun violence into the pulpit. I was leading worship at a Korean-American church in Richmond when news broke of the shootings at Virginia Tech in Blacksburg. I remember the fear and the uncertainty as many in the congregation had friends and family members attending the university at the time. Years later, I preached a very similar sermon after Gabrielle Giffords was shot and six others killed in Tucson. I preached another such sermon after Aurora, and then Sandy Hook. I even preached about guns not two months later, after my uncle decided to put a pistol to his head and pulled the trigger. I've preached that sermon many, many times over the last ten years of my ministry, and you know what has changed in that decade? Nothing. Absolutely nothing. Each episode follows a familiar pattern. There will be a public outcry for the days and weeks following the massacre. People, pundits and pastors will get on the television and wag their fingers, blaming the tragedy on this and that and the other. Political parties will spar and bicker attempting to gain a few points in the polls and after a while, almost like clockwork, it will all simply fade away—just as it always does.

And I used to say this in my sermons—It sounds almost naïve now, but I used to say, "These barbaric acts that sick and misguided persons inflict upon our communities are an aberration to normal society. They are not normal. We can take some measure of comfort in the knowledge that such terrible acts can still shock us." But now, I'm not so sure I can use that line anymore. Can anyone honestly tell me that they are surprised this has happened again? It becomes increasingly evident how we have grown numb to the presence of gun violence in our communities, especially as we simply kick the proverbial can just a little further down the road, waiting for the next tragedy to occur so we can pretend to be appalled again. Since I entered seminary thirteen years ago, there have been over 400,000 firearm-related deaths in this nation, 8% of which (roughly 30,000) were children.[3] If those numbers happened anywhere else in the world, we would decry it as genocide; we would shake our fists in moral outrage and cry aloud in righteous indignation. Yet as it happens in this nation, nothing changes, and all people of faith can seem to do is offer more thoughts and prayers. Well, with all due respect to Father Gutiérrez, if that's not, "disinterested religion", I don't know what is!

As I alluded to in my sermon last week, the act of prayer is meant to be empowering, the purpose of prayer is to inspire action among the people of God, not to exercise meaningless pleasantries designed to placate our burdened conscience. Now, I don't know what the solution is for gun violence in this nation; I have my opinions just like anyone else. But the numbers don't lie—*the status quo is wholly unacceptable, not to mention morally repugnant.* How often has, 'The devil made him do it,' become our excuse for public cowardice? We can try to blame Satan all we want, but perhaps we need to come to terms with the idea that maybe Satan isn't the real problem here. If we can fix the problem, and we refuse, this makes us accomplices at the very least. And when I encounter empty catch-phrases like, *"Three Things that Make America Great: God, Guns and Guts"*, tragedy forces me to the realization that we possess far too much of one and are severely lacking in the others.

What makes a nation great? If tens of thousands of people *did not* die every year due to firearms—if we belonged to a society where violence was not seen as the solution to our problems—if mental illness was not stigmatized and people could get the help they needed—if we enjoyed a functional political system that could set aside petty ideologies long enough to work together to accomplish something...*anything*! Now *that* would make for a truly great nation! But that is not who we are—not now—or, as we commonly say, "Not again..."

To echo the lamentation of Job, where is God during tragedy? Well, I'll let you in on a little secret. In situations like those in Roseburg, Sandy Hook and Columbine, God is not with the guns; God is squarely in the line of fire. God is among the suffering who must pick up pieces of their shattered lives because of our collective indifference. I wonder, how many more chapters of this human tragedy will we be forced to sit through before we arrive at any kind of resolution? We can do what Satan expects of us and merely give in to easy temptations of cynicism and apathy, or we can do something exceptional. We can demand more of ourselves, we can demand more of our church, and we can demand more of our leaders. We can trust God by allowing God to work through us, not just by accepting the bad, but by laboring toward the good. For when it comes to creating meaningful transformation in the world, the odds may not be in our favor, nevertheless, God is always betting on us to do what is right. In Jesus Christ, the Lord has put, "skin in the game" for our sake. Can we do no less? Who knows, perhaps someday we might pay off!

Blessing and glory and wisdom and thanksgiving and honor and power and might be to our God forever and ever! Amen.

1. Newsom, Carol, *The New Interpreters Bible: Job*, Vol. 6, p.347-348, Westminster John Knox Press, 1996
2. Gutierrez, Gustavo, *On Job God-Talk and the Suffering of the Innocent*, pg.5, Orbis Books, 1987
3. www.cdc.gov

Although Mark is my favorite gospel, I do have tremendous appreciation for the Gospel of Luke. As the new liturgical year gets underway in "Year C" of the Revised Common Lectionary, we focus our attention to the Christmas story as seen through Luke's eyes. I often refer to Luke as, "The Revolutionary Gospel", because of the wide-ranging implications for the world which come as a direct result of Christ's presence among us. Born into a world of power and privilege, the mere mention of this child's name along with that of the Emperor of Rome brings into question everything we think we know about power and lordship. With the Nativity, Luke lays the foundation of his entire gospel story, presenting us with a universally inclusive vision of the Good News as it escapes its humble confines in Palestine and radiates out to the four corners of the known world, welcoming all people into a renewed covenant community of grace, hope and love. And as this new world is being built, this means the old order of power and privilege is slowly fading away.

Topsy-Turvy

1 In the fifteenth year of the reign of Emperor Tiberius, when Pontius Pilate was governor of Judea, and Herod was ruler of Galilee, and his brother Philip ruler of the region of Ituraea and Trachonitis, and Lysanias ruler of Abilene, ²during the high-priesthood of Annas and Caiaphas, the word of God came to John son of Zechariah in the wilderness. ³He went into all the region around the Jordan, proclaiming a baptism of repentance for the forgiveness of sins, ⁴as it is written in the book of the words of the prophet Isaiah, 'The voice of one crying out in the wilderness:

*"Prepare the way of the Lord,
make his paths straight.
⁵Every valley shall be filled,
and every mountain and hill shall be made low,*

> *and the crooked shall be made straight,*
> *and the rough ways made smooth;*
> *⁶and all flesh shall see the salvation of God.'"*
>
> Luke 3:1-6 (NRSV)

Many years ago, during my junior year of college, I was having the absolute worst day. A recurring bout of bronchitis had forced me to drop out of a required physical education class, and I had to spend an entire afternoon traversing the brick-laden walkways throughout the campus of North Carolina State University on a bureaucratic wild goose chase, trying to collect the necessary signatures from professors and doctors which would allow for a medical deferment, so that dropping the class wouldn't count against my grade point average. In the course of trying to secure one such signature, I had been blessed out by an arrogant associate dean (for reasons which still escape me), and as I made my way up Hillsborough Street fuming while replaying the incident in my mind, one of the grizzled homeless men standing outside Bruegger's Bagels shouted to me, "Hey, Man! God loves you! He told me to tell you that."

An odd blessing, for sure, but as far as timing goes, there could not have been one better. Who knows why this man said what he did at the moment he did? Perhaps he had a tenuous grasp of reality, he might have been "self-medicating," or perhaps he was just fishing for some loose change. All of these could be indeed possible, and yet what he said when he said it made me consider the fact how God is present in my life, even throughout those bad days when everything appears to go wrong. This encounter made me appreciate for a brief moment in time, that regardless of my class standing or my grade point average or the stresses and strains of everyday life, I still belonged to a God who loved me, and who had the strangest and most wonderful ways of reminding me of the many ways in which I have been blessed.

Tradition holds that the writer of the Gospel of Luke was a physician. However, I prefer to think of Luke as a playwright. And unlike many of my other theories, I don't believe this one to be particularly far-fetched. One notices a certain poetry to Luke's writing. Scholars like to point to Luke's clinical and polished tone as proof of the author's vocation, yet I have discovered as much art as science in these pages. Luke weaves elegant patterns and parallels within the gospel, and imbues those pages with a conscience for the human condition that is found nowhere else in scripture.

It is not like the rough-hewn character of Mark, nor is it like crankiness of Matthew or the spiritual detachment of John; in many ways, the gospel of Luke marks a journey throughout time and space which leads the reader from Christ's humble origins in Nazareth, through the cross in Jerusalem and eventually into the halls of power of Rome itself.

By the third chapter in Luke's Gospel the prelude of the Nativity has passed, and so the gospel broadens its focus. *"In the fifteenth year of the reign of Emperor Tiberius, when Pontius Pilate was governor of Judea, and Herod was ruler of Galilee, and his brother Philip ruler of the region of Ituraea and Trachonitis, and Lysanias ruler of Abilene, during the high-priesthood of Annas and Caiaphas…"* Now, Luke is not merely stating things this way to offer us the precise year that these events occur; he is also describing the world into which Christ was born. All of the characters who will play such a significant role as the story unfolds are present and accounted for as Luke carefully sets the stage upon which this drama of Christian faith will take place. *Caesar* is at the top, then Pilate, then Herod, with Annas and Caiaphas in the high priesthood. It is the structure of a society based upon the politics of power, patronage and enforcement of the status quo. This hierarchy insists that there is a certain order to be maintained in this world, and it is spelled out for us in clear detail. Should one ever venture into this political landscape, then make no mistake, pilgrim! This is who is in charge. Caesar, Pilate, Herod, Annas, Caiaphas—these are the major players of the world that is.

Enter then what would appear at first to be a minor supporting character. Enter John the Baptist; an itinerant preacher traveling from place to place invoking the ancient prophets and proclaiming baptism and repentance for the forgiveness of sins. John comes from the *opposite* direction of this world that is. He doesn't come from the rank and file of Temple mount or the walls of Jerusalem or the halls of power in Rome; he walks straight out of the wilderness—the harsh, arid landscape of the Palestinian desert. He could not have come from farther away from these "powers that be". The Gospels of Matthew and Mark describe him as wearing a tunic made from camel hair, eating locusts and wild honey. Icons from ancient Christian traditions portray him with dark, matted hair and sporting a gnarly, twisted beard. Try to imagine for a moment how someone like John must have appeared to people of that time, espousing prophecies of bizarre harvests and coming baptisms of fire. Or, let me put it this way: What would you think if you encountered someone like that today? You would more than likely just assume he were a crazy person, someone who lives far upon the fringes of what polite society might consider acceptable.

Yet already in the Gospel of Luke, there is an odd tension that is beginning to develop, which will challenge our expectations of what's normal or not. Compare the eccentric personality of John the Baptist (one whose sanity must have been in question even way back when) dressed in dirty and smelly clothes, living off the land, spouting forth prophecy, fire and brimstone. And yet, within the words of that prophecy comes the promise of a new hope as John proclaims the establishment of divine justice and a new way for people to relate to God and one other. Compare this seemingly insane man to Caesar, Pilate, Herod, Annas or Caiaphas—persons upon whom the whole social structure rests. These are respectable people…educated people…*powerful* people—and yet (as we will come to know from history and the gospels witnesses), these are the people who are willing to inflict great horrors upon others to maintain and expand their personal power. These are the people who would slaughter mere children to protect their crown. These are the people who would willfully condemn an innocent person for the sake of political expedience. So, this begs the question: Who is the real crazy person in this story? Is it the one who testifies to the real and immanent presence of the divine, or is it those who view human life as a mere commodity to be traded at their own convenience?

Every holiday season, Myra and I set aside time to watch the classic Christmas movie *Miracle on 34th Street*. If you've seen it, then you probably know where I'm going with this. In the movie, you have an older gentleman who is gentle and wise, generous and kind-hearted. There just appears to be one problem: He thinks he's Santa Claus! And the more he speaks and acts like Santa Claus, we begin to wonder, for after a while, he starts to appear suspiciously like the real thing. Yet because other characters feel threatened by his kindness and spirit, they go to great lengths to expose him as a fraud. Thus, a similar question is presented to the audience: What is the definition of insanity? Is it the kindly man who believes himself to be Santa Claus, or is it those who oppress and exploit the most vulnerable among us to compensate for their personal inadequacy?

This may explain why John had to retreat to the wilderness to begin with, so that he might escape from this oppressive and volatile society of Caesar, Herod and Pilate—a place where human life was cheap, and it was considered socially acceptable to cast judgment and withhold mercy. Perhaps the harshness of the rocky, desert terrain was far less severe than what might have been considered "normal" at the time. Rather than wear the robes of a corrupt priesthood, John chose the hair of a camel; rather than feasting upon the labor of others, John chose to eat what the land provided; rather than maintaining the manicured appearance of a noble, John chose to reject the falseness and arrogance of outward appearances. Perhaps it was only by living in silence and isolation among God's creation that he could truly listen to the voice of the Lord.

With the return of John the Baptist from the wilderness, this carefully laid out social structure which has existed for hundreds of years immediately gets turned upon its head. The prophet has come to testify to a new reality, the advent of a new Kingdom with God as Lord—a kingdom where divinity and power are no longer held captive in the hands of an elite few; rather John declares that *all flesh*—all people everywhere shall bear witness to the presence of God. *"Prepare the way of the Lord!"* John declares. Move aside Caesar and Pilate; Herod, this means you, too! Your power is mere illusion. Might no longer makes right. Justice will never again be dispensed by the sword. Honor and glory are no longer a by-product of your office. In this new world, only humility before God and repentance from sin provide the true measure of righteousness. The voice of John the Baptist heralds the advent an era where everything is different now, a time when even creation itself becomes transformed in anticipation of the divine.

And as we all know from the rest of this story, these leaders from Caesar, to Pilate, to Herod, to the chief priests—all of them will reject this new reality. None of them will find the courage within themselves to cast their lot into an uncertain future in which they are required to place their trust in something over which they hold no control. Not only will they choose to reject this new reality, they will use every means at their disposal to resist it, to destroy it, and to crush it with all their might. They will mock it and beat it; they will hammer it high upon a cross and drive spears into its side; they will bury it in the ground and cover it with a stone and forget all about it. And yet, in the ultimate twist of irony, the act that they believe will subdue it forever is the very act that provides its final victory.

Although the life of John the Baptist may have long since come and gone, the call of the prophet does not diminish with time. The same voice that spoke so long ago still speaks to us today, and this declaration is not simply a message for the Caesars or Herods or politicians of the world, but a call for all people everywhere to recognize the presence of the divine in our midst—to have the courage to admit our human failings and place our to trust in the mercy and forgiveness of the Lord. How have we prepared the way for the Lord? How are we making room for creative avenues of possibility through forgiveness, compassion and reconciliation?

Often in our lives, we will run across people who will come to us from outside of what might be considered acceptable. They will come from poverty; they will come before us with matted hair or gnarly beards, uttering strange phrases which seem to make little sense. Their appearance will make us uncomfortable; they will make us want to run away and hide in the safety and comfort of exclusivity and isolation. But with the advent of Christ, the mountains of our pride have been laid low, the valleys of our fears have been filled, and the crooked ways of our hearts have been made straight. Simply put, there is no longer any place to hide from the coming of the Lord. The poor, the homeless and all who suffer invite us into community with the divine, to remind us of the endless possibilities God's steadfast love. They call us into action to help those in need, and as God's people, we are obligated to respond.

The cry of John the Baptist declares to all who will listen that the time of our personal isolation has ended. The time of deprivation has passed. The prophet has moved out of the wilderness and among the people where a new ministry of repentance and humility begins. Now is the time in which the Lord will live among God's people. No longer is this a time for scarcity. Now is the time for abundance—an abundance of compassion, an abundance of forgiveness, and an abundance of love—and the time for sharing that abundance has arrived.

Blessing and glory and wisdom and thanksgiving and honor and power and might be to our God forever and ever. Amen.

Christmas is perhaps the most difficult time to preach. It's not that I find the slightly above average crowds intimidating…No, it's hard because you are preaching from the same few texts again and again and again. Don't get me wrong, these are lovely passages which people look forward to hearing each year (including myself), and it just wouldn't be Christmas without them! But at the same time, how much juice can you squeeze out of that orange? So, the challenge for the sermon-writer is: How can I keep the story fresh? How can I see the same familiar story through a new set of eyes?

When I am in desperate need of inspiration, I always turn to the prophets. Prophetic literature engages the reader on many levels, simultaneously speaking to history, current relevance and future hope. Isaiah's vivid, powerful language lends itself to bold storytelling. Although the exercise of divine justice weighs mightily in the prophets' words, at the same time, they also bear the seeds of a new hope proffered by a faithful God. This teaches us how the two are not mutually exclusive; indeed, God's wrath is an extension of God's mercy. Through the prophets, God establishes familiar patterns of divine behavior, assuring the people of God that God's promises for Israel are not just a remembrance of former glories, but God's redemptive activity is still occurring very much in the present.

Promises, Promises

> *2 The people who walked in darkness have seen a great light; those who lived in a land of deep darkness on them light has shined. ³ You have multiplied the nation, you have increased its joy; they rejoice before you as with joy at the harvest, as people exult when dividing plunder.*
>
> *⁴ For the yoke of their burden, and the bar across their shoulders, the rod of their oppressor, you have broken as on the day of Midian. ⁵ For all the boots of the tramping warriors and all the garments rolled in blood shall be burned as fuel for the fire. ⁶ For a child has been born for us, a son given to us; authority rests upon his shoulders; and he is named Wonderful Counsellor, Mighty God, Everlasting Father, Prince of Peace. His authority shall grow continually, and there shall be endless peace for the throne of David and his kingdom. He will establish and uphold it with justice and with righteousness from this time onwards and for evermore.*
>
> Isaiah 9:2-7 (NRSV)

I think it's fair to say that Christmas and movies go hand in hand. From

Miracle on 34th Street to *It's a Wonderful Life*, we all have our feel-good favorites. One phenomenon I've noticed lately is an influx of "Hallmark" Christmas movies that dominate the cable airwaves around this time. The cable guide description will read something like this: *"Candace Cameron Bure is a high powered attorney who loses her corporate job and starts a new practice in a small New England town, where she falls in love with Greg, a local ski instructor, who works the mountain over the Christmas holiday to make ends meet until his hand-crafted furniture business gets off the ground. (Also, starring Jane Seymour as Greg's over-bearing mother.)"*

It's brain candy for the masses for sure, but that's okay, because our expectations are somewhat modest to begin with. Sometimes you want to see, "an intellectually gripping, visually stunning, emotional 'tour-de-force'", but other times, you just need a happy ending. Now personally, I cannot bring myself to admit whether I like the Hallmark Christmas movie or not, but I can certainly respect it for what it is. It fulfills a need, sometimes unapologetically so. I get most upset when a movie misrepresents itself, or fails to live up to expectations. Obviously, there's not much danger of that happening with a Hallmark movie.

Never do we feel as let down as when things fail to live up to our expectations, and Christmas is no exception. We recall former times with such fondness and nostalgia, that when the holiday season finally rolls around, we make grandiose plans that are hard to live up to. And yet something always happens: Someone can't make it, the food doesn't turn out the way we hoped, or perhaps the kids want to spend time with their friends. We become crestfallen when things fall short of what we had envisioned. This doesn't make us bad people, we're only human after all; our reach often exceeds our grasp. Yet when it comes to the holidays, it takes great discipline to avoid comparing reality to what we have built up in our imagination.

The book of Isaiah was written during the most turbulent time in the history of the people of Israel. Yet throughout it all, the prophet's words testify to a new hope and the fulfillment of God's promises. These bold promises would be embodied in the form of a Messiah, a child born to lead the people of God out of the darkness and into the light, a new king to rule with justice and righteousness. Isaiah's words anticipate with celebration the day when the fortunes of Israel would be restored, the bonds of oppression broken, and the tools of war burned so that they might be used no more.

Needless to say, expectations for this Savior were quite high. And over the centuries, the people of Israel would build up in their imagination a Messiah according to what they wanted, rather than how God would see fit to provide. Many would imagine a great military conqueror who would overthrow foreign occupiers. Others envisioned a new prophet, a new Elijah to rain fires of judgment upon Israel's enemies. Still others wanted the heir to King David who would bring untold riches and prosperity to God's people. *"Wonderful Counsellor! Mighty God! Everlasting Prince of Peace!"*

That's a lot to live up to, for sure. When we consider the enormous expectations placed upon this Messiah, only then do we understand how Jesus never really stood a chance! When people expected great rewards, Jesus told them to forsake material possessions. When people demanded that Jesus cast judgment upon sinners, Jesus instead forgave them. When people expected a conqueror, Jesus instructed them to love their enemies. This obviously didn't sit very well with people who wanted the king, the prophet or the warrior as *their* Messiah. Jesus defied every single expectation such people had for him, and in the end, they crucified him for it! But then Jesus continued to defy expectations by rising from the grave, proving the truth of his words—there is power in vulnerability, prestige in humility, and liberation in servitude. Endless riches are to be gained by living in genuine love and fellowship with God and one another. Indeed, the salvation of humankind entered into the world, not through some mighty act of power, but from the cries of a lowly infant echoing from a cattle trough.

We must remember that the Christmas season is a time of *anticipation*, not expectation. That is why we celebrate the coming light of Christ in the world by anticipating what Christ expects from *us*. We are called to serve the Lord, not the other way around. Yet even to this day, people still place unrealistic expectations upon Jesus. People want a Messiah to validate beliefs, rather than challenge them. We want Jesus to prove that *I* am right and *they* are wrong, that *I* am righteous and that it's *those others* who are immoral, that *I* am saved and *I deserve* to be rewarded for my faith. But Jesus instead comes before us to remind us once again that the grace of God does not work according to our expectations, for the same undeserved grace that redeems those sinners over there happens to be the same grace that redeems this sinner right here!

You see, that's the thing about being led from darkness into the light; we see things with a lot more clarity. We can look around and see the many ways in which God is at work in the world. We can see the promises fulfilled through the kindness and compassion of ourselves and others, but at the same time, this doesn't mean we just get to see the good stuff. This new and clearer vision allows us to see the many ways that we continue to let our God down. We can see the hungry and homeless on the streets. We can see the lonely, the addicted and those who suffer. We can see those who are ostracized or oppressed. We can see our own harshness reflected in our arrogance and selfishness—wasted opportunities for reconciliation caused by apathy or complacency. We can see the countless ways that we continue to crucify Jesus Christ on the cross of our expectations, and entomb the grace God within hearts of cold stone.

Yet again and again Christ proves that he does not fit so neatly inside of a box. Jesus is still running loose in the world, healing bodies and freeing minds. Moreover, his power is such that even our own sinfulness may be transformed to serve God's ultimate purpose. Jesus Christ is, at the same time, the promise kept and the promise given. Emmanuel remains out in the world, bringing light to those who live in darkness, while charging the Lord's disciples to do the same.

Blessing and glory and wisdom and thanksgiving and honor and power and might be to our God forever and ever. Amen.

As a pastor, I still get questions about whether it is permissible for Christians to consume alcohol. This is always a tricky subject. Scriptural witness is not much help, because it is all over the place on the subject. On the one hand, I'm convinced that there is no act more Christian than simply gathering around a table to share a drink with friends. But at the same time, I have to temper that enthusiasm by acknowledging the very real dangers of overconsumption, as well as the detrimental effect alcohol and substance abuse has on both individuals and families. We must be sensitive to the nature of addiction and how it can prevent one from full participation in the fellowship of the church, because human nature reveals an ugly truth: We're all addicted to something. The same could easily apply to other forms of human weakness which hold us back from serving God completely. Some of these can be easily overcome, while others prove quite daunting. So, what is it that hold us back? Is it our fear? Our job? Our relationships? Our need for adulation? Or possibly even our faith? What obstacles must be overcome so that we may fully commit ourselves to life in true community? With a love which transcends our limitations, Christ comes among us to remove that which restrains, so that we might become the life of the party!

[Please drink responsibly.]

The Good Stuff

1 On the third day there was a wedding in Cana of Galilee, and the mother of Jesus was there. ²Jesus and his disciples had also been invited to the wedding. ³When the wine gave out, the mother of Jesus said to him, 'They have no wine.' ⁴And Jesus said to her, 'Woman, what concern is that to you and to me? My hour has not yet come.' ⁵His mother said to the servants, 'Do whatever he tells you.'

⁶Now standing there were six stone water-jars for the Jewish rites of purification, each holding twenty or thirty gallons. ⁷Jesus said to them, 'Fill the jars with water.' And they filled them up to the brim. ⁸He said to them, 'Now draw some out, and take it to the chief steward.' So, they took it. ⁹When the steward tasted the water that had become wine, and did not know where it came from (though the servants who had drawn the water knew), the steward called the bridegroom ¹⁰and said to him, 'Everyone serves the good wine first, and then the inferior wine after the guests have become drunk. But you have kept the good

> wine until now.' ¹¹Jesus did this, the first of his signs, in Cana of Galilee, and revealed his glory; and his disciples believed in him.

John 2:1-11 (NRSV)

Our scripture lesson today is very near and dear to my heart. You see, this is the scripture Myra and I chose to be read at our wedding. Yet curiously enough, despite the setting, it's not a passage people commonly associate with weddings. We're the only couple that I know of who has done so. Often, people opt for more popular passages, "*Love is patient; love is kind; love is not envious or boastful…etc. etc.*", or the classic, "*Therefore what God has joined together, let no one separate…*" I suppose I can appreciate why this passage from John's gospel is not terribly popular for such an occasion, after all, there are no romantic musings about love or selfless devotion, or the responsibility and sanctity of marriage. When we do some across Jesus at this wedding in Cana, he is apparently involved in an argument with his mother, which is not exactly something anyone wants at their wedding. Yet like any wedding, this is a passage full of distractions, and even the characters who witness these events first-hand struggle with their significance.

Miracles can be a little distracting. When we read the stories of Jesus' miracles in the Bible we are presented with things that seem too good to be true. They are difficult for otherwise rational people to accept. And as a result, people often become quite divided over whether such events occurred in history. When Myra and I visited Cana as seminary students, there were a variety of churches and shrines scattered about the city, each claiming that this was the *actual* site of Jesus' miracle. So much energy and expense was invested into establishing proof, that one could easily become jaded and dismiss such stories as mere fable and fantasy. Yet as I have mentioned before, miracle stories in scripture are neither history nor fantasy, nor were they ever intended as such. They are not meant to convince us of anything, rather they intend to teach us something about God.

As we read the story, Jesus takes water from containers that have been reserved for a Jewish purification rite and miraculously transforms it into wine. Now, the rite for which the water was set aside can no longer take place. Through this miracle, Jesus teaches his followers, that in the Lord's eyes, celebration is a far worthier offering than rigid observation of the law. With the power of God working through him, Jesus is able to turn something old into something new; he takes something ordinary and transforms it into something extraordinary. Jesus presides over the creation of a new covenant, one that is not based upon ritualistic observance, but rather one centered upon the love that we can only discover by living in true relationship with God and one another. Before his miracle, the reception was about to come to an abrupt halt and people were about to go their separate ways, but now with this miraculous transformation, this celebration of love and fellowship may go on without end.

Very often in life we find ourselves falling into familiar patterns in how we relate to others. We stick to our comfort zone: We surround ourselves with people who are like ourselves, who believe in the same things we believe in, who work in the same field, who vote for the same political party, etc. etc. After a while, these patterns constitute a ritual by which we increasingly isolate ourselves from those with whom we do not share much in common. But Jesus showed through his miracle that the old ways of doing things are no longer sufficient. We are called by God to live in genuine love and fellowship with everyone, not just those groups with whom we feel most comfortable. We have to embrace new attitudes and new ways of thinking, new ways of reaching out toward others through compassion and common understanding. Only by remaining open to the possibility of transformation and change can we perform miracles of our own every day.

What drew Myra and I to this passage was not the miracle, nor necessarily any profound theological meaning. What we loved most about it was the simple idea of Jesus being present at a wedding. Indeed, Christ's presence is vital to any form of Christian celebration, whether it is at a wedding or a baptism or even when we get together informally as a church to share a meal every now and again. Whenever we gather in genuine love and fellowship with one another, then the presence of Jesus Christ is made real, not in some abstract theological sense, but in very profound and meaningful ways. Nowhere else is this more typified than when we partake of the Lord's Supper together. I know that at least according to Presbyterian tradition, the Eucharist has evolved into a somewhat somber and introspective affair, but it is at heart, the Lord's Supper is intended as a celebration of Christ's presence among us. This is symbolized by the physical presence of the bread and the wine at the table, the same wine that was shared at the Last Supper, the same wine that was made evident at Jesus' very first lesson, through which we are united as a community of faith.

I often wonder what that Lord's Supper would look and feel like if we really did treat it as a celebration. With commotion and cheer, with shouting and laughter, with loud music and dancing—not just a pinch of bread here and little cup of grape juice there, but with countless loaves of fresh bread and endless bottles of fine wine—something akin to what we experience at a wedding reception surrounded by family and friends (but perhaps leaving out the ugly bridesmaids' dresses). The bread and the wine would flow forth with joyful abandon just as they did so long ago. Wine represents the beating heart of the Christ's new covenant: Excitement…revelry…*possibility*. The old covenant was like jars of water—I mean, sure, you can get by on it, but where's the fun in that? Through Christ's presence, the cups of all present overflow with joyful abandon. There is so much wine that to keep it from going to waste, people *must* share it with others. I can imagine the crowds from the wedding spilling out into the streets and alleyways of Cana to welcome others into this celebration so that they too may share in the blessing of this newfound abundance.

When Myra and I were in seminary, our theology professor, Doug Ottati, used to hold a, "Theology Discussion Group" every Friday evening at one of the local watering-holes. The two of us were regulars at such fellowship, and at one gathering, a new first-year student came in wearing a t-shirt which sported the declaration, "No Thanks, I'm Trying to Get into Heaven." The slogan on the shirt revealed an unfortunate, yet all-too common error among many Christian circles today that treat the grace of God as a finite resource—something that must be carefully rationed out only to those who somehow manage to prove themselves worthy. ("Here's some for you…here's a little for you…but oh no, *not for you*!") However, the presence of Jesus Christ in our midst testifies to a new reality, where the grace of God overflows in tremendous abundance, an open invitation for all who are willing to partake of it by joining in the celebration and fellowship that has been so generously provided.

One thing you will hear me say time and time again is that Christianity is not, nor has it ever been about scarcity. We do not earn salvation or redemption based upon those little things which we choose to deny ourselves. God is not some petty deity who needs to be appeased through ritual acts of self-deprivation. The Christian life is the opposite of this. The Christian life is about abundance—an abundance of faith, an abundance of compassion, an abundance of forgiveness, and most of all…*most importantly of all*…an abundance of love! Moreover, we are charged by the Lord our God to share our abundance with others, even if we have to venture out into alleyways and streets of our community to find them. Now *that* would something else—one might even say, *miraculous*.

I would be remiss if I did not take a brief moment to acknowledge the upcoming Martin Luther King, Jr. holiday, where we take a day out of the year to commemorate one who was willing to give everything he had for the cause of God's righteousness and justice. King saw fundamental civil rights and the alleviation of poverty in America as not just an African-American cause, but a struggle for the rights and dignity of all people, including who King frequently called his, "white brothers and sisters". Too often, when we offer of ourselves to God or to one another, we only think in terms of what is practical, pragmatic or prudent. Therefore, in this modern age, when we encounter people of different races, religions or cultures, we hold "tolerance" up as the noblest of ideals, because that is all many of us are willing to give. And don't get me wrong: tolerance is good, tolerance is fine…you can get by on it, sure. (But seriously, how many of you look forward to receiving that Hallmark card in the mail which reads, "Dear so-and-so: I *tolerate* you.") As people formed in the image of God and as disciples of Jesus Christ, we are called to aspire toward something greater. Our goal is not tolerance. We are not called to merely "tolerate" one another's differences, but to honor and bless that which makes us so special and unique. Through Jesus Christ, we share in the knowledge that each of us lives in this world as a beloved child of God, and as such, we are called to gather in joy and celebration as *one family* into the presence of our Lord.

Can such a miracle occur? Sure, why not? Stranger things have happened. It was in speaking of miracles that a famous pastor by the name of William Sloane Coffin once wrote:

> *"Miracles do not a messiah make. But a messiah can do miracles. If you ask me if Jesus literally raised Lazarus from the dead, literally walked on water and changed water into wine, I will answer, 'For certain I do not know. But this I do know: faith must be lived before it is understood, and the more it is lived, the more things become possible.' I can also report that in home after home I have seen Jesus change beer into furniture, sinners into saints, hate-filled relations into loving ones, cowardice into courage, and the fatigue of despair into the buoyancy of hope. In instance after instance, life after life, I have seen Christ be 'God's power unto salvation,' and that's miracle enough for me."*[1]

Blessing and glory and wisdom and thanksgiving and honor and power and might be to our God forever and ever. Amen.

1. William Sloane Coffin, *Credo*, p.10, Westminster John Knox Press, 2004

I've always found John Calvin's views on free will particularly fascinating, as they reflect a more mature understanding of human behavior relative to God's providence. Although Calvin would acknowledge that all human beings sin voluntarily, he would insist that this does not mean our will is "free". For Calvin, free will was something which existed before the Fall of Adam, when human beings still possessed the ability to distinguish between good and evil. However, original sin destroyed this ability, to the extent that human will can only choose what is evil, making decisions based upon self-interest and personal desire, instead of God's commandments. As we are unable to manifest goodness in and of ourselves, our only hope is to turn to God for guidance and mercy. "Therefore, though all if us by nature the same disease, only those whom it pleases the Lord to touch with his healing hand will get well…whatever righteousness, holiness, piety and purity we can have are gifts of God."[1] By that token, faithfulness is not measured according to personal virtue, but in our willingness to persevere in hope and trust, remaining open to the transformative presence of the Spirit, so that divine goodness and mercy may be free to act through us according to God's will. To God alone belongs the glory!

This sermon will win me no friends among the Baptists or Methodists, but some things just need to be said.

Ready or Not…

4 Now the word of the Lord came to me saying,[5] 'Before I formed you in the womb I knew you, and before you were born I consecrated you; I appointed you a prophet to the nations.'

[6]Then I said, 'Ah, Lord God! Truly I do not know how to speak, for I am only a boy.' [7]But the Lord said to me, 'Do not say, "I am only a boy"; for you shall go to all to whom I send you, and you shall speak whatever I command you.

[8] Do not be afraid of them, for I am with you to deliver you, says the Lord.' [9]Then the Lord put out his hand and touched my mouth; and the Lord said to me, 'Now I have put my words in your mouth.
[10] See, today I appoint you over nations and over kingdoms, to pluck up and to pull down, to destroy and to overthrow, to build and to plant.'

Jeremiah 4:1-10 (NRSV)

Choice…In my humble opinion, if ever there were a "four-letter-word" in the history of Christianity, it would be "choice". (Relax, I know it's literally six letters; my arithmetic is not *quite* that bad.) How this insidious little word ever introduced itself in the tradition of Christian belief, I will never know. Never mind the fact that the world "choice", or "choose" occurs very rarely in scripture, and when it is used, it has very little to do with our human capacity to decide one way or another. Nevertheless, you don't know how many times in my ministry that I've had a pastor or other individual frequently inform me of the choices I need consider. "You have a *choice*," they will say. "You all have a choice to make in this life. You have to *choose* to accept Jesus Christ. You have to *choose* between good and evil."

Now, I know that they mean well, but really, how did things get to be as simple as picking between only two potential outcomes? Makes it seem easy! That's as simple as flipping a coin. 50/50…Hey, I like those odds. If that were a hand of poker, I'd go all in! But I often wonder, what is it? What is it about our human nature that makes us believe we have choice in this life? Where do we find assurance in such an idea? What is it about our ability to choose that offers us such comfort? Is it a byproduct of the highly individualized modern-day consumer culture in which we live? Is it trying to live up to this idealized image of the, "self-made man" we've created for ourselves? What makes us assume that in the grand cosmic scheme of history, something as wondrous, mind-boggling or indescribable as eternal salvation could be left to something as fragile or as fickle as human *choice*?

Even if we truly possessed the ability to choose good from evil, or right from wrong in this world, then the world is inherently unjust. If it just so happened that we were all born into the same life and in the same life situation, if we all started at the same place at the same moment in history, then *maybe* something like choice might make a little more sense. But that is not how things have worked out. Some people are born into very supportive and loving families, while others are born into environments of struggle and neglect. Some people are born into poverty, and others born into prosperity. Some in this world appear to have an infinite amount of choices available to them, while others possess very few. Is that fair? Is that justice? In reality, who we are and the decisions we make seem, not so much determined by matters of choice, but more by patterns of necessity—factors of environment and heredity—boundaries set forth by nature and nurture that push and pull us in one direction or another. Most of us here have been blessed to live in abundance, never having to worry about where our next meal was coming from, therefore, what right do we have to judge a starving person who has to steal food to survive?

You see, now…now we're starting to get at the heart of why we human beings demonstrate such a preference for choice. Choice is a luxury. Choice is entitlement. Choice is *power*. Choice allows us to tell ourselves that if we are successful, happy, respected and loved, that means we are good people because we made all the correct decisions in life. On the other hand, if someone happens to be struggling in theirs, it is because they have made very bad choices, hence, they are by extension a bad person! Choice justifies us in our own eyes and provides the illusion that everything, even something like eternal salvation is somehow within our control. And why? Because if we can control *that*, we can control anything, for we believe…we honestly believe our fate is better off in our hands. Trust no one. Leave it all up to myself and myself alone. After all, who else is more qualified to look after me, but me? What makes you think that I can simply trust someone else to provide direction and purpose for my life?

Choice is a luxury. However, given the present state of the world, I for one believe it to be a luxury that we cannot afford. After all, given the "choice", how often do human beings chose what is best for us? No, no…given the choice, we will almost always choose what we think is in our personal interest. Given the choice, we will prefer to disregard the needs of others. Given the choice, we will look the other way in matters of injustice, while blissfully reveling in the rewards of influence and affluence. Don't rock the boat. Keep things just as they are. Ironically, many of the choices we do make end up limiting the choices of others. "Sorry buddy, I've got mine…You're on your own!" Yet the many souls in this world neglected to addiction, hopelessness, poverty, homelessness and despair daily serve as living testaments to our human capacity to choose.

If you will notice, when the Word of the Lord first comes upon the prophet Jeremiah, the idea of "choice" never enters into the equation. The Lord does not advise Jeremiah, "You know Jerry, you really should consider going to all whom I send you or (I don't know) maybe possibly think about speaking whatever I command you…that is, if you think you have the time." No, Our God is never that wishy-washy. God commands Jeremiah, "You **shall** go to all to whom I send you, and you **shall** speak whatever I command you." Now, you tell me, where is the choice in such a declaration?

Oh, don't get me wrong, like any one of us, Jeremiah is never short of excuses. We may not have much of a choice in the matter, but we still have it within ourselves to resist the will of God. Our fears and our insecurities aim to get the better of us, seeking to turn us away from the tasks to which we as God's people have been appointed. "I am only a boy," Jeremiah cries. "I am too weak…I am too small…I am too insignificant to make a real difference in the world. Let me just stay here in my comfort zone where it's safe and where I promise never to bother anyone."

Likewise, we offer up similar excuses, "Maybe some other time, God. Maybe when I feel better prepared. I'll forgive my enemies later. I'll love my neighbor later. I'll give to the poor later. I'll feed the hungry later. I promise…I'll get around to it eventually. I'll wait until that moment when I am ready to live according to your will." To which the Lord quickly answers, "You have *no excuses*, and you have no such luxury, because you, like Jeremiah, you specifically have been appointed to accomplish the Lord's intentions. Doing the will of God is not a choice, but a divine *command* to love one another with a radical, self-giving love. *You—you* have been formed with purpose and right intention to play a part in God's ultimate plan for the entire universe! Now given *that*, how small or how weak or unprepared could you possibly be?

Well, I suppose I should take a step back. Actually, there is "choice" in the Christian faith, but not as we might assume. As I mentioned earlier, the words "choose" or "choice" are used very rarely in scripture, but when they are, seldom do they have anything to do with our ability to choose one way or another. It is not we, but God who chooses. The word "choose" is far, far more often used to describe what God does for us—that God has chosen us from all the peoples of the earth to be holy and to love and serve our Creator. This is echoed in the words of the Apostle Paul, when he states that the gifts given to us by the Holy Spirit are allotted as the Spirit chooses. Even Jesus emphatically states in the Gospel of John, "*You did not choose me, but I chose you. And I appointed you to go and bear fruit, fruit that will last…*" [15:16]

No matter how young or how old, how weak or how strong, how rich or how poor, everyone in here has the power within them to obey the will of God, just as each of us has the ability to resist the Lord's intentions. And the simple fact is, no one is capable of making good decisions 100% of the time, as we are equal beneficiaries of a common grace. In the grand scheme of cosmic history, it is God who chooses, just as it is God who determines and destines. God's inevitable purposes shall be fulfilled one way or another for creation, often in spite of our obstinacy to the contrary. We can act in concert with that plan as God has intended us to do, or we may frustrate this plan as we are able. Yet regardless of our rebelliousness and in spite of our fears and insecurities, the power of God is such that it is strong enough and capable enough of having our disobedience serve God's purposes as well. So, given that there is no real choice in the matter, we may want to think more seriously about getting on board with the program, because, as the prophet tells us, the Lord is coming whether we are ready or not!

In other words, being a bigot is not a choice. Being a racist or a misogynist is not a choice. Hatred of others is not an option. You cannot place the empty pursuit of wealth over the needs of your neighbor. You are not allowed the luxury of looking the other way in the face of injustice. God has declared that there is no choice in such matters. In acting as such, we only prove ourselves to be slaves to sin and a living testament to our brokenness. Still, so many people in this world not only see this as their choice, but their God-given right! Nevertheless, those who build themselves up the highest—those who seek to elevate themselves above others—the judgment of the Lord will strike them *first* when it falls from the heavens!

On the other hand, serving the will of God is an obligation not to be taken lightly. And yet in spite of Jeremiah's fears and reservations, God assures Jeremiah that the Lord will be with him. And so, the reluctant prophet accepts the calling to which he has been appointed, for the Lord promises to always stand with those who possess the courage for the task. *"Now I have put my words in your mouth,"* says the Lord. *"Today I appoint you over nations and over kingdoms, to pluck up and to pull down, to destroy and to overthrow, to build and to plant."* God declares that *now* is the time to do the dirty and difficult work of the gospel.

There exists an odd contradictory nature within the call of Jeremiah, that he is called to destroy and to pluck up on the one hand, but asked to build and to plant on the other. And whereas the two images may not make sense with one another, nevertheless, there is great comfort in the renewing power of God's Word as it tears down former ways of living and believing so that faith and love may be built upon a stronger foundation, or, clearing the fields of weeds and rocks so that a harvest of righteousness may be sown in abundance. These instructions may not seem to fit so neatly together on the surface, yet there is purpose and meaning in these apparent contradictions. In much the same way, obedience to God's will which can often seem so confining and restricting is actually the means by which we gain perfect freedom through Jesus Christ our Lord.

One might easily make the argument that the most important decisions in life are best not left in our hands, but in God's. After all, children seem to fare far better when they are presented with an *illusion* of choice. For instance, some of the best parents that Myra and I know don't ask their children, "Do you want to eat your vegetables?" rather they ask, "Would you prefer to eat carrots or peas?" The question would not be, "Do you want to wear your coat?" but rather, "Would you like to wear your blue coat, or your brown coat?" In spite of the limitations imposed upon them, children at least feel somewhat empowered by this illusion of choice that will, in the long term, assist them in growing up to become mature adults. So, I suppose, when it comes to those things that are best for God's children, perhaps the best choice, is no choice whatsoever.

Blessing and glory and wisdom and thanksgiving and honor and power and might be to our God forever and ever. Amen.

1. Calvin, John, *The Institutes of the Christian Religion, II. v. 3 & 8*, ed. John T. McNeill, Westminster John Knox Press, 1960

An intriguing facet of Luke's gospel is how Jesus and his disciples are in perpetual motion. There are always traveling somewhere, even if we don't quite know where that is at this point in the story. The constant wandering presents us with somewhat of a mystery: Do they even know where they are going? Is there some destination to which they have been called? After literally walking around in circles for the first eight chapters of the Gospel of Luke, we find Peter, James and John taking refuge with Jesus high upon a mountaintop, where the divine light of Christ is suddenly and miraculously revealed. One might assume that the Transfiguration would mark the climax of the story, and that everything which follows would be descending action. And yet barely one verse later we find Jesus and the disciples back on the road again, doing the mundane work of the gospel while moving toward something else. In times when I feel stuck, I take great comfort in a Christ who is constantly in motion for our sake, one who goes to tremendous lengths to close the distance between the Lord and humankind.

[An early draft of this Transfiguration sermon was entitled, "Light Up & Get High with Jesus", which I think we can all agree is totally inappropriate. I shall do my penance in due time…]

What Goes Up

28 Now about eight days after these sayings Jesus took with him Peter and John and James, and went up on the mountain to pray. 29 And while he was praying, the appearance of his face changed, and his clothes became dazzling white. 30 Suddenly they saw two men, Moses and Elijah, talking to him. 31 They appeared in glory and were speaking of his departure, which he was about to accomplish at Jerusalem. 32 Now Peter and his companions were weighed down with sleep; but since they had stayed awake, they saw his glory and the two men who stood with him. 33 Just as they were leaving him, Peter said to Jesus, 'Master, it is good for us to be here; let us make three dwellings, one for you, one for Moses, and one for Elijah'—not knowing what he said. 34 While he was saying this, a cloud came and overshadowed them; and they were terrified as they entered the cloud. 35 Then from the cloud came a voice that said, 'This is my Son, my Chosen; listen to him!' 36 When the voice had spoken, Jesus was found alone. And they kept silent and in those days told no one any of the things they had seen.

37 On the next day, when they had come down from the mountain, a great crowd met him. 38 Just then a man from the crowd shouted, 'Teacher, I beg you to look at my son; he is my only child. 39 Suddenly a spirit seizes him, and all at once he shrieks. It throws him into convulsions until he foams at the mouth; it mauls him and will scarcely leave him. 40 I begged your disciples to cast it out, but they could not. 41 Jesus answered, 'You faithless and perverse generation, how much longer must I be with you and bear with you? Bring your son here.' 42 While he was coming, the demon dashed him to the ground in convulsions. But Jesus rebuked the unclean spirit, healed the boy, and gave him back to his father. 43 And all were astounded at the greatness of God.
Luke 9:28-43 (NRSV)

Our scripture passage for today is a play in two acts. The first act, is of course a scene that we may already be familiar with; the scene of Jesus' transfiguration on the mountaintop; the physical revelation of his divine glory before his disciples. This is an important event in our liturgical year, and just as we do Christmas, Easter and Pentecost, we always set aside time every year to pay homage it. Obviously, this annual Christian observance will never be quite as popular as those others I mentioned, (I have yet to receive my Transfiguration present) but it is important nonetheless. But why, I cannot exactly say. Even though we celebrate the Transfiguration of Jesus Christ every year, I'm not sure that I have ever come across an adequate explanation of what the Transfiguration is, or what it truly means.

Commentaries and sermons I've read seem to dodge the issue altogether by saying scholarly things like, "The Transfiguration affirms Jesus' place in the prophetic tradition of the old testament..." or "Jesus' experience on the mountaintop is a summation of the entire gospel..." These are all well and true perhaps, but there seems to be more than mere allegory going on in this scene. There actually appears to be no clear purpose to it whatsoever. It is not a response to something; it just occurs out of the blue. Although one could easily describe the Transfiguration as miraculous, it doesn't fit the technical definition of a miracle. There's no particular lesson to be gleaned here. The Transfiguration only reveals what we pretty much already know by now in the Gospel of Luke, that Jesus is not just a good teacher, nor is he a mere prophet. Events are happening here that go far beyond our human understanding of who Jesus is and the relationship he shares with the divine.

But then again, maybe that's exactly what is being articulated here. In many ways, his unexplainable transfiguration speaks of the very mystery of

Christian faith itself, so perhaps we shouldn't feel at a loss simply because we can't fully grasp what's going on. Indeed, the disciples who bore witness the Transfiguration first-hand struggle with its significance.

Take Peter, for instance. He tries…he means well…but it becomes quite clear from the story that he doesn't quite understand what's going on here. Peter is presented with the very revelation of the Lord's divinity upon the mountain, and he arrives at the erroneous conclusion, "You know what? We should set up shop here! We should build three homes, one for Jesus, one for Moses and one for Elijah, and we can live here. We can spend our days communing with the divine, revealing the glory of God for worthy souls willing to make the journey to this place." And it's not like Peter is being unreasonable. Surely the words of the prophet Isaiah echo through his mind, "*In days to come…the Lord's house / shall be established as the highest of the mountains…Many peoples shall come and say, / Come, let us go up to the mountain of the Lord, / to the house of the God of Jacob; / that he may teach us his ways / and that we may walk in his paths.*" [2:2-3] Peter dreams that the homes they build will mark the foundation of a new city dedicated to the glory of God. He imagines that right here…right here on this very spot is where God's Kingdom of which Jesus speaks will finally begin.

It's no mystery that mountains are very special to Jesus in the Gospels. They are places of prayer and spiritual renewal, a refuge from the crowds who surround him. We who live in the Shenandoah Valley understand the many blessings of such beautiful landscapes. Yet no matter where we hail from, there is something about the mountain which calls to each of us. There is something about being isolated from the sounds and the stresses of daily life, able to appreciate the natural beauty of God's creation and to see well off into the distance. From on high we can see the burdens of life on a proper scale when measured against the sheer magnitude of the rock, where time has little power or meaning. The mountain is where we may place ourselves above it all to think and reflect amid stillness and silence. And just as it is for us, so it was for Jesus as well. The mountain does not worry about the presidential election, or keeping a job, or making the mortgage payment, or saving for kids' college tuition, or the stock market or terrorist threats—the mountain simply *is*.

And barely two verses later, the stillness of the mountain is shattered, and we find ourselves in the next scene back among the crowds of people shouting and screaming…A jostling mass of humanity which clamors for Jesus' attention. "Jesus! Jesus! Come quick! I need you!" "My father has a crippled leg and cannot walk…" "Jesus, I am going blind…lay your hands upon me." "Jesus! Jesus! How can my soul be saved?" "Jesus, I am hungry, give me something to eat?" "Jesus, my wife is dying…" "Help me, Jesus! Help me!" Truly Jesus must have been completely overwhelmed by this much human need. Finally, one man approaches Jesus and says, "Jesus please help my son…he is suffering from seizures. You're the only person who can help me…please help!" And then Jesus does something which is…well, rather unJesus like. He scolds the assembled crowds shouting, "*You faithless and perverse generation, how much longer must I be with you and bear with you?*"

Now it is unclear who exactly Jesus is scolding here. Is it the man? Is it his disciples? Is it the crowd? All of them? All of us? Regardless, it is obvious that Jesus has lost all patience with those who surround him. Perhaps this is one of those scenes in scripture where Jesus' human side makes itself apparent. As Christians, we do not often think of Jesus experiencing things like frustration, anger or fear. We have a tendency to imagine Jesus as above it all, detached from cumbersome and unpredictable human emotions, and yet our passage clearly indicates otherwise. But really, can you blame him? Just a few moments ago Jesus was communing with the divine amid the tranquility and natural majesty of his mountain refuge, and now he finds himself neck-deep in a flood of mortal affliction. So much hunger…so much disease…so much pain… For all of his divine power and wisdom, there seems to be little that even Jesus can do in the present.

And certainly, the future must have weighed heavily on Jesus mind as well, for what Jesus spoke of on the mountain with Elijah and Moses was not of divine wisdom or knowledge or spiritual enlightenment, but rather the conversation was of his coming crucifixion and death. All of tension, all of this frustration and fear suddenly boil over in a fit of rage in the midst of this noisy crowd. For all these many people who demand so much from Jesus now will soon abandon him to die alone in the company of criminals. These people clamor so loudly for attention will be the same ones who taunt him as he hangs upon the cross, "If you're so high and mighty, why don't you just *save yourself?*"

Now, by this time in Luke's Gospel, Jesus was certainly no stranger to temptation. He had already matched wits with Satan, the master of temptation himself, and come out three-for-three. And just when he thinks he's finished with such nonsense, here it comes again, from Peter of all people! Truly Jesus must have been tempted by Peter's offer, to build a home upon the mountain and to live there, far removed from the screaming masses below, where he may live in quiet contemplation and solitude. What a life he could have had away from those who demand so much of him, secure from the dangers and machinations of his adversaries. But Jesus understood that he could not reconcile God and humanity living as a monk on a secluded hillside; accomplishing the will of God meant coming down off the mountain, getting among the people and helping others—doing the real work of the gospel—feeding the hungry, healing the sick, easing the pain of those who suffer. What a joy it would have been to live a comfortable and safe life far removed from this ungrateful world. How easy it would have been to simply hide away—to turn a blind eye to a desperate humanity while avoiding the pain and humiliation of the cross.

Often when people get angry or frustrated, our natural inclination is to lash out, or perhaps worse, to simply give up. When confronted by the many social problems of this world, the easiest solution is to separate ourselves from it, to ignore it in the vain hope that it will merely go away. We leave the poor, the sick and the hungry to their own devices, and find new ways of blaming them with the claim that their suffering is somehow their own fault. The seemingly endless demands of a world in need frustrate us to the brink of surrender. And yet this lesson illustrates the true difference between Jesus and the people around him. Despite his frustration, anger and fear, Jesus does not hide from the tasks to which God has appointed him. He sets his volatile emotions aside to do what needs to be done. He heals the boy of the father who asks him, just as he will continue to do the will of God even at the cost of his very life. Think about that for a moment: When Jesus becomes frustrated and angry with us, he gives this son back to his father healed and whole. Yet when humanity becomes frustrated and angry with Jesus, we return him to his father bleeding and bruised, battered and broken through the many crucifixions that Christ is again and again forced to endure in this world.

In life, we endeavor to distinguish ourselves among our peers and in our community in a multitude of ways, and these are noble and worthy pursuits, but with personal success, we run the danger of isolating ourselves from our fellow human beings. We can receive a first-class education, we can move into a higher tax bracket, we can accumulate a great deal of power and influence in our community, we can even have great spiritual experiences which defy all human understanding, each of which seem to place us above others high upon a mighty mountain of our own making. And like Peter suggests, the temptation is to stay up there—to live the easy life of affluence and influence, to associate exclusively with others who enjoy similar elevated status, far above the frustrations and fears which afflict the rest of society.

But Jesus shows us the true gravity of discipleship: What goes up, must come down. A refuge is not our escape from the world, rather it is a place where we may renew ourselves for the difficult work to which the Lord has appointed us. A refuge is a place where we may seek to hear with greater clarity the voice of the Lord calling us to God's service. Jesus knows that the kingdom of God will never be found secluded high upon a mountaintop; it can only be discovered within our common humanity, through the sharing of our gifts and strengths, with humble acknowledgment of our limitations and weakness. The kingdom can only be truly experienced through kindness and compassion—the many sacrifices we must be willing to make as we confront challenges posed by poverty, hunger, disease and suffering. And to do this, we need to be able to stand on even ground to look one another in the eye.

Will this work be frustrating? Absolutely. Will it make us angry? Most definitely. Will it make us afraid? Count on it. No one said it would be easy, least of all Jesus. But these perfectly natural emotions of frustration and anger and fear that we naturally experience prove no barrier to our service when we follow the example of Christ. When we do as the Lord instructs and listen to him, we can witness a transformation within ourselves as God's glory becomes revealed to the world, and we too may be astounded by the greatness of God.

Blessing and glory and wisdom and thanksgiving and honor and power and might be to our God forever and ever. Amen.

If you will notice, I try to keep my sermon titles short. We are a traditional Presbyterian congregation here at First Waynesboro, so the possibility of having a LED digital marquee is a remote prospect at best. (It's just as well, as I would likely abuse the privilege.) Positive staff relations are an important part of our ability to function effectively. Since my administrative assistant is the one who assumes responsibility for changing letters on the church sign outside on 11th Street, it is vital that I remain in her good graces, especially during those blustery, Shenandoah Valley winters. Therefore, we have settled upon an unspoken accord of sorts, whereby I keep the lettering to a minimum, and she remembers to put my paycheck in my mailbox, instead of under the photocopier. For this, we are each grateful. Therefore, if just a small amount of consideration can inspire feelings of gratitude and thanksgiving, just imagine the blessings which can stem from living within a covenant community of grace and love!

Split Decision

1 After these things the word of the Lord came to Abram in a vision, 'Do not be afraid, Abram, I am your shield; your reward shall be very great.' ²But Abram said, 'O Lord God, what will you give me, for I continue childless, and the heir of my house is Eliezer of Damascus?' ³And Abram said, 'You have given me no offspring, and so a slave born in my house is to be my heir.' ⁴But the word of the Lord came to him, 'This man shall not be your heir; no one but your very own issue shall be your heir.' ⁵[The Lord] brought [Abram] outside and said, 'Look towards heaven and count the stars, if you are able to count them.' Then he said to him, 'So shall your descendants be.' ⁶And [Abram] believed the Lord; and the Lord reckoned it to him as righteousness.

7 Then [the Lord] said to [Abram], 'I am the Lord who brought you from Ur of the Chaldeans, to give you this land to possess.' ⁸But [Abram] said, 'O Lord God, how am I to know that I shall possess it?' ⁹[The Lord] said to him, 'Bring me a heifer three years old, a female goat three years old, a ram three years old, a turtledove, and a young pigeon.' ¹⁰[Abram] brought him all these and cut them in two, laying each half over against the other; but he did not cut the birds in two. ¹¹And when birds of prey came down on the carcasses, Abram drove them away.

12 As the sun was going down, a deep sleep fell upon Abram, and a deep and terrifying darkness descended upon him.

17 When the sun had gone down and it was dark, a smoking fire-pot and a flaming torch passed between these pieces. 18 On that day the Lord made a covenant with Abram, saying, 'To your descendants I give this land, from the river of Egypt to the great river, the river Euphrates..."
Genesis 15:1-12, 17-18 (NRSV)

As the fifteenth chapter opens in the Book of Genesis, we find the future Hebrew patriarch Abram (later known as Abraham) back in the land of Canaan after yet another long and arduous journey. It was while residing far in the east, the Word of the Lord comes upon Abram, son of Terah, instructing him to take his family and his possessions westward into the land of Canaan.

Once there, God promises to Abram that the land upon which he now resides would be given to Abram's descendants. Ever since God made this promise, however, Abram and his family have always been on the move, and it would appear as though they would never quite be able to settle down long enough to make their home. Famine would soon cause Abram and his wife Sarai (later Sarah) to leave Canaan to venture to the land of Egypt, then after that they would wander eastward to the Negeb, and then finally once again back into Canaan. Yet after walking the length and breadth of the land, Abram would then have to travel north past Damascus to rescue his nephew Lot, whose family had been taken captive after a battle between local warlords.

But even so, all of this movement was actually the least of Abram's concerns. The Lord had, promised the land of Canaan to Abram's descendants, and yet at this point in the story, Abram still has no heir. It was a situation made even more complicated by the fact that Abram and Sarai were already quite advanced in age, far beyond one's typical child-bearing years. It would stand to reason that if the land of Canaan was, according to the Lord, to be given to Abram's descendants, first and foremost, this would require a descendant to which to give. Thus, our scripture lesson from Genesis this morning begins with a rather terse, yet highly understandable complaint by Abram who says, "O Lord God, what will you give me, for I continue childless?"

Two chapters earlier, God reiterated the promise God had made, informing Abram that his descendants would be, "like the dust of the earth." [13:16] But this time, God directs Abram's gaze upward to the night sky. "*Look towards heaven and count the stars, if you are able to count them."* God says to Abram, *"So shall your descendants be."* Now we have to bear in mind what this sky looks like at this time. This would not be like the skies we are familiar with in the 21st century, congested with light and atmospheric pollution so only the brightest of constellations are able to peek their way through the haze. In the dry, arid landscape of a preindustrial sky, no doubt the heavens were illumined by an infinite multitude of stars of every brightness, every intensity, every size and every color streaming outward from the bands of the Milky Way, a sight which must have overwhelmed Abram's senses as his dizzy gaze attempted to move from one star to the next. And who knows? Perhaps the sheer wonder of the cosmos— the near impossibility of the infinite creation he saw before his eyes convinced Abram of God's ultimate intentions for him and for his family. Thus, it is mentioned that Abram put his trust in God, *"and the Lord reckoned it to him as righteousness."*

To drive this point home, what follows in the next scene is an odd ritual of sorts, the full meaning of which has largely been lost to time. The next evening, at the Lord's instruction, Abram sacrifices a series of animals, and then divides the carcasses in two, creating two piles of remains, one on his left and one on his right. Back in Abram's time, this was seen as the initiation of a blood oath. To seal a contract between two people, the parties involved would walk between the divided remains, signifying that if either violated the agreement, the culprit would be doomed to suffer a similar fate. Yet this evening as the night sky descended once again, something extraordinary would happen. After Abram has fallen into a deep sleep, we the readers bear witness as God passes through the remains *alone*, signifying to Abram and to all creation God's willingness to endure death so that God's promises can be fulfilled. And so, it is at this very moment, God formally establishes his covenant with Abram, *"To your descendants I give this land, from the river of Egypt to the great river, the river Euphrates…"*

What does it mean to live in a covenant relationship with God? Again, perhaps this also is something of which the full significance has been lost to time. After all, we live in such a litigious society today, as we have entire industries dedicated to keeping our promises to one another through various legal and technological means. Our experience in the modern world narrows our gaze to the point that we cannot appreciate the full meaning of what it means to live in covenant. To us a covenant is a contract, by which each party is charged with the responsibility of upholding their respective end; you give a little, I give a little and everyone benefits. Yet the covenant we share with God is decidedly one-sided. As the heirs of Abraham, we share a deep and abiding trust that God will be our God and we God's people.

Living in covenant with the Lord means knowing that God keeps God's promises. If there is one lesson to be learned from all scripture, it is precisely that. Yet in our lesson today, God dramatically demonstrates the extraordinary lengths that God will go to uphold this covenant, for even though we're the ones who routinely violate this bond when we fail to live and act as the people of God. Even though we show a propensity to neglect justice, ignore compassion and forsake the needs of others, nevertheless, the Lord again and again proves willing to singlehandedly assume the burden of those consequences. Through this ritual, God demonstrates the nature of the covenant we share in tangible terms—a covenant in which God and humanity both agree to participate. Yet it is also through this ritual that we bear witness to a God who not only knows our sacrifices, but also sacrifices along with us, and most importantly, sacrifices *for us* on *our* behalf, testifying before the vast universal cosmos and all of creation that we are never alone.

And even though we live in a far different time and place, like Abram, we still find ourselves to be a people on a journey guided by God's promises, and like Abram, it can often appear at times that we are just wandering around in circles with very little progress to show for it. When we see the many horrors, we inflict upon one another either through intent or neglect, when we see our future or the future of our children in doubt, when we a world overwhelmed by human suffering, during those times when God appears absent or unconcerned with the things which threaten us, we also complain to God with that familiar mixture of bewilderment, anxiety and frustration. "How long?" we cry. "How long before you make good on your promises? How long must we wait before you usher in your reign of righteousness and peace? When, God, when? I'm waiting!"

As much as I loathe the practice of sharing catchy nuggets of pop-culture wisdom in the course of my sermons—and as much as I hate to admit it— every now and again something will catch my attention. Many of you may have come across this anonymous quote which has been circulating throughout the internet of late, which says, "*Sometimes I want to ask God why he allows poverty, famine, and injustice in the world, when he could do something about it…but I'm afraid he might ask me that same question.*" And as we consider this covenant relationship that we share with our Lord, we must also bear in mind how we are called to be participants in this ritual of God's grace. Like anything genuine and worthwhile, it is a relationship which requires sacrifice. We have to use our hands to get down to the messy and sometimes bloody work of discipleship, so we may prepare that space for the Lord's presence to pass through, opening our hearts and minds to place trust in God's infinite mercy and steadfast love. And very often that presence will come upon us invisibly, silently, when we are least aware, nevertheless our willingness to participate is still reckoned as righteousness.

As I am always saying, many people misunderstand the act of faith. We think of faith as possessing perfect piety, spotless morality or passionate religious zeal, but truth be told, at its heart, faith is actually none of these things. Faith in God and trust in God's promises are best expressed through *perseverance*…persistence…keeping our eyes fixed upon the faraway horizon with the determined knowledge that in spite of our weaknesses, in spite of our many shortcomings, we can still live and act as God's people, because God's promises to us *have been, will be and are being fulfilled!* And whereas in the course of this journey we may struggle to keep our promises to God, this does not mean we cannot do a better job of keeping our promises to one another!

When we come upon Jesus in the Gospel of Luke, his adversaries, the Pharisees, have some rather dire warnings for him as he wanders throughout Judea teaching and healing the people. With a counterfeit concern for Jesus' safety, they say to him, *"Get away from here, for Herod wants to kill you."* And hearing this, Jesus boldly replies, *"Go tell that fox for me, I am casting out demons and performing cures today and tomorrow and one the third day I will finish my work."* [Lk. 13:32] The tasks to which Jesus has been appointed are never once driven by the fears of an uncertain future, rather he occupies himself with the needs of the present—how God is calling him to live and to serve in genuine concern for the here and now—gathering his children as a mother hen gathers her meandering brood. In spite of our many anxieties and trepidations, God is still keeping God's promises, as they have been sealed through a sacrifice of unfathomable grace and love. All the many Herods of the world are powerless to prevent God's creative intentions. Moreover, together we may rest assured that through Jesus Christ, God has set the stage whereupon the drama of salvation will take place at the proper time and place of God's choosing. In the meantime, there's work to be done!

Blessing and glory and wisdom and thanksgiving and honor and power and might be to our God forever and ever. Amen.

If there's one good thing about this job, you know you'll never starve to death. Like all churches, First Waynesboro has our fair share of pot-luck dinners and meals for special occasions. Food has always been a necessary element of Christian worship and fellowship. The simple act of gathering around a table to share in a communal meal forms our understanding of what it means to be the church. And yet as impactful as this can be for the church of today, in ancient times it was even more so. In a modern era filled with grocery stores, taco trucks and drive thru restaurants on every block, we find ourselves far removed from cultures where hospitality was not just simply regarded as an act of kindness, it was a matter of survival! Indeed, the patriarchs of the Old Testament, the Apostles and even Jesus himself understood the value of true hospitality. Unfortunately, mutuality and trust are often the first casualties of this increasingly suspicious and individualized age in which we live. Although times change, people change and cultures change, some things must remain constant, lest we lose sight of our basic humanity. Although they may assume different forms, elements which lie at the heart of who we are should be regarded as sacred (or as some might say, "sacramental"). How can we as the Christian community restore a culture of hospitality, whereby we come to recognize, and even celebrate, our dependence upon God and one another?

Somebody should really be compensating me for this kind of corporate endorsement. I'll look for my check in the mail, Mr. Easterbrook!

All You Can Eat

1 Ho, everyone who thirsts, come to the waters; and you that have no money, come, buy and eat! Come, buy wine and milk without money and without price.
²Why do you spend your money for that which is not bread, and your labor for that which does not satisfy? Listen carefully to me, and eat what is good, and delight yourselves in rich food. ³Incline your ear, and come to me; listen, so that you may live.

I will make with you an everlasting covenant, my steadfast, sure love for David. ⁴See, I made him a witness to the peoples, a leader and commander for the peoples. ⁵See, you shall call nations that you do not know, and nations that do not know you shall run to you, because of the Lord your God, the Holy One of Israel, for he has glorified you.

⁶Seek the Lord while he may be found, call upon him while he is near; ⁷let the wicked forsake their way, and the unrighteous their thoughts; let them return to the Lord, that he may have mercy on them, and to our God, for he will abundantly pardon.

⁸For my thoughts are not your thoughts, nor are your ways my ways, says the Lord. ⁹For as the heavens are higher than the earth, so are my ways higher than your ways and my thoughts than your thoughts.

¹⁰For as the rain and the snow come down from heaven, and do not return there until they have watered the earth, making it bring forth and sprout, giving seed to the sower and bread to the eater, ¹¹so shall my word be that goes out from my mouth; it shall not return to me empty, but it shall accomplish that which I purpose, and succeed in the thing for which I sent it.

¹²For you shall go out in joy, and be led back in peace; the mountains and the hills before you shall burst into song, and all the trees of the field shall clap their hands. ¹³Instead of the thorn shall come up the cypress; instead of the brier shall come up the myrtle; and it shall be to the Lord for a memorial, for an everlasting sign that shall not be cut off.   Isaiah 55:1-13 (NRSV)

We've all experienced it before. On occasion, you'll get hungry and find yourself at the counter at McDonald's, looking over the menu. Not that there's anything wrong with McDonald's; Lord knows many a Quarter Pounder has met its demise at my hands, but maybe you're having one of those weeks when fast food is the last thing you want to eat. Maybe you've been especially busy with work and have been forced to eat only quick meals on the go, or perhaps you've spent a lot of time traveling in unfamiliar environs. And so, you stand there in line, staring blankly at the menu above the counter looking for something different to try this time, or perhaps wondering if that leftover Chinese food from last week is still good. So reluctantly, you step up to the counter and place your order, and after grabbing your tray, you make your way to your seat, pausing for a brief moment to sigh over your food before summoning up the courage to take the first bite.

But glancing up for a moment, you notice a young family across from you. A mother and a father, just starting out in life, having a night out with their five-year-old son and three-year-old daughter. And the kids…well, as they say, "They're lovin' it." With his head just perched up above the table the boy grasps his cup with two hands and drinks his coke in due haste, while the former contents of his happy meal lie strewn across the table surface. After finishing his drink, he skips off with his father in tow to the ball bin in the playground. All the while, the little girl laughs with delight with half of a French fry dangling from her mouth. I mean, you can easily think of a hundred other places you would rather be eating, but for these kids, this is the greatest thing in the world. McDonald's is the pinnacle dining experience if you are a child. There is nowhere else in the world these kids would rather be right now.

I suppose the older we get, we begin to lose something. Things in life which once seemed exciting and new to us as children begin to lose their luster with time. Perhaps even some of us can remember a time when we too laughed over our McNuggets with joyful abandon. But unfortunately, time, that ever present thief in our lives, seems to come along and steal many of these small, yet precious moments from us. It happens; we just get older. We turn sixteen or seventeen, we get our driver's license, and then we can pretty much get McDonald's anytime we want. The novelty quickly wears off, we find new restaurants that we like better, or we have a bad experience and refuse to go back. Over time, those little things that delighted us so much when we were younger slowly become routine and dull by comparison, and after a while we take them for granted. Or perhaps we come to see ourselves as above certain experiences— been there, done that, and so on. ("McDonald's? Gross! I wouldn't be caught dead eating there!")

But suppose for a second, word got out early tomorrow morning that McDonald's was giving out free food all day. Who do you suppose would be the first in line? Well, it probably wouldn't be those people who only eat McDonald's when they feel like they have no other choice, no— more than likely it would probably be the poor, and the hungry, and those families with young children who would quickly fill up the lines at the counters with orders for Big Macs, milkshakes and happy meals. The lines from the counter would overflow out the door and into the street with the people who love it, who need it, and those who feel as though they just can't live without it.

Jesus describes one such a feast in the gospel of Luke. Speaking to the scribes and Pharisees one day, he says, "*Someone gave a great dinner and invited many. At the time for the dinner he sent his slave to say to those who had been invited, 'Come; for everything is ready now.' But they all alike began to make excuses. The first said to him, 'I have bought a piece of land, and I must go out and see it; please accept my regrets.' Another said, 'I have bought five yoke of oxen, and I am going to try them out; please accept my regrets.' Another said, 'I have just been married, and therefore I cannot come.' So, the slave returned and reported this to his master. Then the owner of the house became angry and said to his slave, 'Go out at once into the streets and lanes of the town and bring in the poor, the crippled, the blind, and the lame.' And the slave said, 'Sir, what you ordered has been done, and there is still room.' Then the master said to the slave, 'Go out into the roads and lanes, and compel people to come in, so that my house may be filled. For I tell you, none of those who were invited will taste my dinner.'"* [Lk.14:16-24]

Now, if you were a Pharisee in Jesus' time, you would hear echoes of the prophet Isaiah in his words. In Isaiah, as in the gospel of Luke, there is a similar invitation extended to everyone to come, eat and be filled. "*Everyone who thirsts, come to the waters; and you that have no money, come, buy and eat! Come, buy wine and milk without money and without price...*" Now, who do you suppose would come to this feast?

When we speak of the Old Testament prophets, the history of ancient Israel profoundly shaped their words and Isaiah no exception. Isaiah is a complicated book in word and origin, one which was curiously written over many years under many different historical and social circumstances, but for the most part, scholars believe that today's passage was written during the time of the Babylonian captivity. That is, the two Hebrew kingdoms of Israel and Judah, which had been strong and independent nations for centuries since the time of King David had gradually ripped themselves apart through forces both inside and outside. Invading armies had torn down the Jerusalem Temple and the citizens of Judah and Israel were banished to the four corners of the Babylonian empire. And these are the people to whom Isaiah is writing; a group of people without a home, refugees condemned to exile.

Indeed, how must have these people thought of their God at a time such as this? Here they were defeated, hurt, angry and humiliated, and there certainly must have been the temptation by many to turn away from their God and toward gods of Babylon or Egypt. They must have thought; look at them and look at us, they are so much more powerful. They have mighty armies, great wealth and endless borders. No doubt many arrived at the conclusion that their nations are stronger, because their gods are stronger; therefore, in order to be stronger, perhaps we should believe in their gods and adopt their ways as well! After all, they have what we want. We want the land, we want the wealth, and we want the power. Our God has obviously failed us. If this is the kind of crud that God is going to be serving me up time and time again, then quite frankly, I don't want any more of it. I should just take my business elsewhere.

But the prophet cautions God's people against such thinking. Isaiah suggests that maybe the kingdom of God will not be like the kingdoms of old. Maybe God's kingdom won't involve great armies, or vast amounts of wealth or secure borders. Money, power, strength; those are the things that we want, those are the things that give us comfort, and those are the things that we think about. Yet as the Lord declares to Isaiah, "*For my thoughts are not your thoughts, nor are your ways my ways. For as the heavens are higher than the earth, so are my ways higher than your ways and my thoughts than your thoughts.*" Therefore, to understand God and to come into God's presence at his table we have to set aside our expectations to trust that there are greater things out there than just the ones we can touch with our hands. Isaiah suggests that the God's people must totally change our way of thinking over what the kingdom of God is like. The kingdom of God will be something beyond our imagination, something far removed from expectation. In this new world, the prophet's words bear the seeds of a new hope, and we are invited, not into the world that is, but into the endless possibilities of what could be.

And so, it is for us. There are many times in our lives where things will not go so well, and it will be we who will suffer in the midst of our own personal exile. Like the Jews in the Captivity, we will feel isolated, defeated, hurt or humiliated afraid, even. Maybe we can't do as much as we used to, maybe we didn't get that promotion we had been hoping for, maybe the person we like doesn't return our feelings, or perhaps even worse, someone we love is hurt or dying. This mortal life that God has given us can seem to lose its luster when compared to how new and exciting everything seemed in more innocent times. As we get older, we become more aware of our sufferings and the sufferings of others, and it will sometimes seem as if God is just shoving that same old, smelly garbage down our throats until it makes us want to vomit. It is times like these when we too will want to take our business elsewhere—we will want to turn away from God, and toward material comforts which offer more immediate gratification. Now don't get me wrong; money, power and influence, when used rightly can accomplish truly great and wonderful things, but how easily we become distracted when such objects reside at the center of our ambition!

It is times like these that we must hear the call of the prophet. We have to reorient ourselves to live as Christ lived, in careful obedience to God's will. Our trust in God is meant to bring us together, and yet still, people use "faith" as an excuse to exclude others. Giving into fear and ignorance, legislatures compose modern-day Jim Crow laws whereby citizens may legally deny goods and services to others based upon one's "religious convictions". Fortunately for us, God has no such reservations, as we have each been invited to God's table with a grace that surpasses all understanding. Our table should be a reflection of God's table. And if you think that having faith means that you should only be in the company of people who look like you, love like you, think like you or believe as you, then perhaps it may be time to reexamine those religious convictions, for the vision of the Good News calls us into *radical* community with one another, bringing people together, rather than driving us apart. At the feast of God's grace, we do not have the luxury to pick and choose who we will dine with, because quite simply, we don't write the guest list. Everyone (yes, *everyone*) is invited to God's table, and proper etiquette dictates that we serve others the way we have been served. Oh, we may not like the company we'll be dining with, but rest assured that those who do respond to God's gracious invitation are the ones who want it, the ones who need it, and the ones who absolutely cannot live without it.

And so, says the prophet, "*so shall my word be that goes out from my mouth; it shall not return to me empty, but it shall accomplish that which I purpose, and succeed in the thing for which I sent it.*" Yes, there are times when we will be tempted to turn away from God, but we can take confidence that God is still preparing a place for us. Unfortunately, when unexpected tragedy occurs, faithful Christians try to rationalize it as "God's will". We've all heard it, "Oh, that's terrible…I feel so sorry for them…well, *it must have been God's will.*" But God does not delight in our suffering; those things that cause us pain in this world are not part of some divine plan. At times like these, even though it is hard, we must remember the lesson God spoke from an empty tomb, that suffering, pain and death are not the final words in life, but the final words in life are hope and love. "*For you shall go out in joy, and be led back in peace,*" says the prophet. Now that—*That is* the will of God.

Living in obedience to God is not easy; it will demand sacrifice—and not by means of petty, meaningless tokens. Sacrifice stands as an expression of gratitude which involves the total reorganization of the self in relation to the world around us. It is a constant evaluation and reevaluation of our lives to recognize the impact that our actions have upon others both across the street and around the globe. It is the reorientation of our hearts, minds, souls and bodies, so we might turn towards God and join our fellow brothers and sisters at this banquet to which we have been invited. And with the power of the Holy Spirit working through us, not only are we transformed, but creation itself becomes altered by its very presence. *"The mountains and the hills before you shall burst into song, and all the trees of the field shall clap their hands… it shall be to the Lord for a memorial, for an everlasting sign that shall not be cut off."*

Bon appetite.

Blessing and glory and wisdom and thanksgiving and honor and power and might be to our God forever and ever. Amen.

This homily was delivered as part of our community Lenten series of worship services, which we do in concert with other churches in the downtown Waynesboro area. It was based upon a sermon I wrote in 2013 after my uncle got drunk one night and shot himself in the head, born from the many thoughts which were racing through my head at the time. Suicide is a particularly sensitive subject in the Shenandoah Valley. A lack of access to mental healthcare combined with an overabundance of firearms, alcohol as well as illegal and prescription drugs, makes for a particularly devastating mix. After delivering this, I was approached by many who expressed great appreciation for the message, as they also had a loved one or a family member who had taken their own life. Suicide is a societal problem which requires a societal response. Tangible answers and concrete solutions will continue to prove elusive as long as we lack the will and the means to act. Admittedly, some Christian traditions and believers might feel as though I'm skating on some very thin theological ice with this message, it is nevertheless vital for the faith community to affirm the sovereignty of a loving and faithful God, especially in times of unexplainable loss.

A Eulogy for Uncle George

> *'The word is near you, on your lips and in your heart' (that is, the word of faith that we proclaim); ⁹because if you confess with your lips that Jesus is Lord and believe in your heart that God raised him from the dead, you will be saved. ¹⁰For one believes with the heart and so is justified, and one confesses with the mouth and so is saved. ¹¹The scripture says, 'No one who believes in him will be put to shame.' ¹²For there is no distinction between Jew and Greek; the same Lord is Lord of all and is generous to all who call on him. ¹³For, 'Everyone who calls on the name of the Lord shall be saved.'*
>
> Romans 10:8b-13 (NRSV)

It was just a little over three years ago, my mother received a phone call in the middle of the night informing her that her younger brother, George had, "died unexpectedly". Now, in this particular case, "died unexpectedly" is a euphemism. For some inexplicable reason that night, my uncle decided that it was a good idea to put a gun to the back of his head and pull the trigger. Although news of his death came as quite a shock, I'm sad to confess, given my uncle's history of alcohol and substance abuse, it was a phone call we had been expecting for some time. In retrospect, I can't even really say that I knew my uncle terribly well. Most of what I remember of him was as a child. Uncle

George was the "cool" uncle. He was always quick with a laugh or a joke at the Thanksgiving table. He was the one who taught me how to shoot a gun, and would drive my sister and me around my grandfather's property in the rusty flatbed of an old, blue Ford tractor. And even though he rarely, if ever, left his home town in his later years, he made an extra effort to come to my wedding, which was noticed and greatly appreciated.

An unapologetic, self-proclaimed redneck in his early sixties, George McManus, Jr. was about six-feet tall sporting rimmed glasses with thick lenses, his greying brown hair pulled back in a ponytail which matched his scruffy white beard. If you ever saw him out roaming the streets of Matthews, North Carolina, he would likely be dressed head to toe in denim in the company of Scarlett, his beloved Great Pyrenees. In his free time, he loved to paint and study black-and white reruns of *The Andy Griffith Show*. He was a voracious reader, and was even known to compose poetry from time to time. Like his siblings, he had a peculiar fascination with *The Wizard of Oz*, and he collected antique editions of Margaret Mitchell's *Gone with the Wind*. Obviously, Country was his music of choice, and almost every night you could find him at the corner bar running the pool tables or strumming away in a jam session on his Martin guitar.

My uncle was eccentric, no doubt, but also highly intelligent and well-read; he was just never cut out for the classroom. As a child, he likely had undiagnosed learning disabilities exacerbated by a botched eye operation which left him nearly blind in one eye. Like many others his age, Uncle George grew up during the counterculture movement of the 60's. He fell in with the wrong crowds and made questionable decisions which would lay the groundwork for addiction. After dropping out of college, he spent his vocational life bouncing from one odd job to next, mostly as a short order cook or bartender, staying just long enough to earn his keep before moving on, yet ironically, never leaving town in the process. He was a fixture in the local community; those who did not know him often dismissed as the town drunk, while many other so-called friends took full advantage of his trusting and loyal nature. My uncle was not what one would consider church-going folk. Although he was baptized a Christian and knew his scripture and catechisms inside-out, as he grew older, he felt increasingly estranged from a church that was largely unwelcoming of his rebellious and nonconformist nature. As such, I'm not really sure how you could characterize his religious views, other than, "discontent".

As far as the 800-pound gorilla is concerned, it's easy to resent the way my uncle ended his life. Suicide can seem such a selfish act. It causes immense pain and heartache, and the person responsible never appears to face any consequences. Those affected can be angry, hurt and confused all at the same time, compounded by the guilt we feel for having such mixed emotions.
Suffice it to say, suicide is traumatic; but is it sinful? I'm not sure we know enough to call it such. Maybe it was the drugs, maybe it was the alcohol abuse, or maybe it was any number of stresses and strains one could point to, but it's clear my uncle was in great pain. And whenever a death like his occurs, people wonder, "What could I have said? What could I have done?" When the truth is, there's little anyone can say or do for someone who is determined to harm themselves. One cannot ascribe rational cause and effect to something which is irrational and unpredictable by its very nature.

As Christians, what should we do with people like my uncle? The way he lived and the way he died provides no shortage of questions. He was not religious, he did not belong to a congregation, nor had he (at least to my knowledge) openly professed faith in Jesus Christ, which could be a problem for some folks. Yet I will personally take great issue with anyone who declares, "Too bad! He had his chance!" Such condemnation presumes much about God, and goes far in placing limits upon God's graciousness and mercy. I do indeed trust in a God of justice; yet I find no justice in condemning someone simply because they didn't, "say the magic words" to our satisfaction. For I am convinced, that if my uncle could find no place in this earthly church—if he could not experience the grace and love of Jesus Christ at work among God's people—then that is a failure in which we all have a share.

In spite of his struggles, my uncle was a gentle soul. He enjoyed a good laugh or a dirty joke. He had a classic "Mac" temper, tenuously held in check by an overburdened conscience. Knowing his own weaknesses, it was never in his nature to judge others. My uncle was at the same time, philosophical and spiritual, selfless and generous of heart. He was the kind of person who would literally give you the shirt off his back if you asked. Indeed, many of his financial troubles arose from simply giving away money to friend and stranger alike. My uncle's faults were many, but they were so often his alone to bear.

Christians today spend so much time and energy obsessing over who is saved and who is damned that it can become quite exhausting after a while. Is heaven so small of a place that there is no room for someone like my uncle?

It the kingdom so exclusive as to become a "members only" club strictly reserved for those in the know? Is grace so weak, so ineffective, that it immediately ceases upon our last mortal breath? As a fellow sinner in the sight of God who is completely dependent upon God for my salvation, I would hope the same steadfast love and grace that is so hard at work on my behalf in life, would be equally so determined in death. We all face temptations in this world. Some of us rise to the occasion and some fall short, but I can guarantee you, no one gets it perfect. To my knowledge, only one person ever has. The moral mileage that appears to separate us from one another is revealed to be mere millimeters when compared to the Lord's righteousness. So, if it truly be God's will, it is my sincerest hope, that in the fullness of time *everyone*—either in this world or the next—*everyone* will come to know beyond the shadow of a doubt the saving power of our Lord Jesus Christ!

You see, that is why Christians possess both a special calling and a special privilege, because we already know this truth! As forgiven sinners, we have seen it; we continue to experience it every day! Through acts of grace and love both big and small, Christ has offered us a "sneak preview" of the world to come. We are blessed with the knowledge that when we call upon name of the Lord, someone is indeed listening, and will go to unimaginable lengths to intercede for us with sighs too deep for words. And because of this, we can have the confidence to endure the hard work of discipleship to bring hope and light to all who live in the darkness of despair.

Though my uncle's death was tragic, I would not consider his life a tragedy. The love and sympathy from those assembled at his funeral was truly humbling. Person after person would line up to speak of how my uncle's life had blessed them, and for my money, that in itself was testimony enough. Yet even though I did not lead the service, I did get to say one last prayer at the graveside:

> *"Lord, it is with confidence in your grace and mercy that we entrust to you our brother George. Bless us now with comfort as we honor his memory. Lighten our hearts with memories of his selfless love and friendship, and as we leave this place today, encourage us to share that love and friendship with others, so that his life with us may endure.*
>
> *Allow us to anticipate that place of which we all dream, where skies are blue and clouds are far behind, where troubles melt like lemon drops away above the chimney tops. That's where we'll find our friend once again."*

Blessing and glory and wisdom and thanksgiving and honor and power and might be to our God forever and ever. Amen.

Rev. John Alexander served as the pastor of my home church of Sharon Presbyterian in Charlotte, North Carolina throughout my young adulthood. His influence was critical in my own decision to pursue a call to ministry. Although he was an excellent pastor and an able administrator, it was John's talents as a preacher which I remember most. His sermons were powerful and provocative, demanding, yet hopeful, and he continues to influence me in ways that I am aware of, but also in ways I can never fully appreciate. John died of Non-Hodgkin's Lymphoma in 2003 at the age of 62 while I was in my first semester at seminary. For someone who didn't grow up having many connections in the greater church, his passing left me feeling somewhat adrift as I gradually reestablished my support system among friends and peers. It made me keenly aware that we can only do what we do in the church because we know how we enjoy the understanding and encouragement of good people. John, like so many others throughout my career, has helped provide a firm foundation of faith from which I could discern where God was calling me!

Letting Go

1 Early on the first day of the week, while it was still dark, Mary Magdalene came to the tomb and saw that the stone had been removed from the tomb. ²So she ran and went to Simon Peter and the other disciple, the one whom Jesus loved, and said to them, 'They have taken the Lord out of the tomb, and we do not know where they have laid him.' ³Then Peter and the other disciple set out and went towards the tomb. ⁴The two were running together, but the other disciple outran Peter and reached the tomb first. ⁵He bent down to look in and saw the linen wrappings lying there, but he did not go in. ⁶Then Simon Peter came, following him, and went into the tomb. He saw the linen wrappings lying there, ⁷and the cloth that had been on Jesus' head, not lying with the linen wrappings but rolled up in a place by itself. ⁸Then the other disciple, who reached the tomb first, also went in, and he saw and believed; ⁹for as yet they did not understand the scripture, that he must rise from the dead. ¹⁰Then the disciples returned to their homes.

11 But Mary stood weeping outside the tomb. As she wept, she bent over to look into the tomb; ¹²and she saw two angels in white, sitting where the body of Jesus had been lying, one at the head and the other at the feet. ¹³They said to her, 'Woman, why are you weeping?' She said to them, 'They have taken away my Lord, and I do not know where they have laid him.' ¹⁴When she had said this, she turned round and saw Jesus standing there, but she did not know that it was

> *Jesus.* ¹⁵*Jesus said to her, 'Woman, why are you weeping? For whom are you looking?' Supposing him to be the gardener, she said to him, 'Sir, if you have carried him away, tell me where you have laid him, and I will take him away.'* ¹⁶*Jesus said to her, 'Mary!' She turned and said to him in Hebrew, 'Rabbouni!' (which means Teacher).* ¹⁷*Jesus said to her, 'Do not hold on to me, because I have not yet ascended to the Father. But go to my brothers and say to them, "I am ascending to my Father and your Father, to my God and your God."'* ¹⁸*Mary Magdalene went and announced to the disciples, 'I have seen the Lord'; and she told them that he had said these things to her.*
>
> John 20:1-18 (NRSV)

When I was growing up in my home church in Charlotte, we had a wonderful pastor named John Alexander. John was a magnificent preacher of the Word who influenced me greatly in my decision to pursue of call to ministry. Yet as with many other influences, I'm almost ashamed to admit that I cannot remember a whole lot about his sermons. I will only occasionally get brief flashes of a memory here or a recollection there, but it's rare when I can remember his words with any significant detail. However, when reading through our scripture lesson from the gospel of John, I rediscovered something which had managed to lodge itself somewhere in the recesses of my brain from one of John's Easter sermons nearly twenty years ago. Whereas attention usually falls upon the image of the empty tomb, or the question, *"Woman, why are you weeping?"* John's sermon on that Sunday morning focused on the seventeenth verse, when the risen Jesus tells Mary Magdalene, *"Do not hold on to me, because I have not yet ascended to the Father,"* which is something that has curiously remained with me all these many years.

"Do not hold on to me..." It seems an odd thing to say, especially in light of the miracle of the resurrection. You might think that he risen Christ would welcome the warm embrace of his closest friends and confidants. This wonderful, glorious thing has been revealed to Mary, and yet Jesus will only allow her to become so close. There is a curious distance the Jesus now maintains between himself and his disciples...so, why?

In his sermon, John proposed that Jesus does not want Mary and the disciples to become too close for a reason. Maybe the risen Christ does not want them to become too accustomed to the memory of that which had come before. With the promise of the resurrection, something altogether new and glorious has unfolded before their very eyes and there is simply no going back to the way things once were. With this new promise that has been revealed, perhaps Jesus wants Mary and his disciples to turn to face the endless possibilities of what could be. Perhaps Jesus understood that by ascending to the Father he would no longer be among them in the flesh, so he wanted them to begin the process of letting go of his physical presence here on earth.

Some years ago, I found myself with a group of pastors, and in the course of a conversation about people of other faiths, one pastor described quote/unquote "moderate" Muslims as those who were, "soft in their faith." He declared that those Muslims who live and work and worship in our country peacefully and lawfully as everyday American citizens…these people are not the "true" face of Islam. Instead, this pastor claimed that the according to the words of the Qur'an, the true face of Islam—those who are truly 'hard' and dedicated to their faith—is best exhibited by the extremists—namely, those terrorists who, "flew those planes into those buildings on 9/11."

Now, as disappointing as his comments were, this pastor's words did manage to drive home a certain point for me, not so much highlighting the weaknesses of Islam, but rather the untold ways in which Christians prove how we are "soft" in our own faith. We affirm our faith in a God, in a Savior who has instructed us to forswear material attachments, a Lord who has quite specifically commanded us to sell what we have so that we can give to the poor and to love one another and our enemies as ourselves—the same Jesus Christ who instructs us to take up our cross and follow him. And yet the pliability of our faith causes us to rationalize Jesus' teachings, to water things down as to make the bitterness of his words more palatable. We think to ourselves, Jesus must just be talking to them, not to me. Jesus can't possibly want us to give up *everything* that we own and everything that we are! Jesus obviously doesn't mean love *everyone*! Jesus cannot demand of us to *literally* take up our cross and follow him all the way to Calvary…Does he?

To determine those who are of the Christian faith, we often ask one another, "Have you accepted Jesus Christ as your Lord and Savior?" When perhaps the question we should be asking is, "What are you willing to give up?" What are you willing to give up to live in God's kingdom of justice, righteousness and peace? Ten percent? Half? All? Because letting go…that's really what it's all about isn't it? That's what it boils down to; our inability as human beings to let go—to let go of our many attachments—those many things in this life which offer us comfort and security. This is what makes us "soft". Who knows why we do these things? Maybe it's in our collective psychology or our DNA. In our hearts, human beings are social animals; we possess this intense desire to belong. We have an almost biological need to surround ourselves with people and things that identify us, or reflect who we are, where we come from, the relationships that we share and the priorities we value. And this yearning to belong that we all share is not necessarily a bad thing. It can actually be a good thing—a source of strength and empowerment—honoring our past and encouraging self-expression in the present. One might even consider such a thing a gift.

But as is so often the case, human beings have a tendency to abuse the gifts we are given. We allow these things—these attachments—to not serve as a reflection of who we are, rather we end up letting these things *define* who we are. We all-too easily become ensnared in a never-ending cycle of avarice fueled by insecurity, where too much never seems enough. We let material objects pile around us, forming a barrier between ourselves and others to the extent that we can no longer see beyond them to witness others in need. We live safe and secure in a little bubble, ignorant of everything and everyone that exists outside our sphere. And the more and more we surround ourselves, the more difficult it becomes to hear the muffled cries of Jesus Christ calling to us to let it all go.

But it's not just about "stuff" or "things", when you think about it, material possessions might be the easiest of which to dispose. It's actually the *intangible* things that prove the most difficult to let go. How often relationships become strained because family and friends cannot let go of petty squabbles or jealousies that happened ages ago? How often we see opportunities for justice and for reconciliation fall by the wayside because people refuse to let go of ancient hatreds and prejudices? How often political and religious differences divide entire communities over what amounts to simple matters of opinion? How often we refuse to let go of our pride that we may truly grow in love and fellowship with our neighbor? How difficult we find it to let go of life's many distractions so we can dedicate just one hour a week to offer thanksgiving and praise to the Lord!

Perhaps most strangely of all, by maintaining this distance from his disciples, Jesus did not want us to get too attached to Jesus himself. I know this sounds weird coming from a pastor. We are taught at a very young age to embrace our Savior with all of our heart, mind and strength. But for those of the

Christian faith, this may be the one single attachment that weighs us down most of all! We weigh ourselves down with expectations of who Jesus should be. We like to declare how Jesus would feel about this issue over here, or how he would have regarded those people over there. We try our best to contain the love and the grace of Jesus Christ in a neat little box labeled, "Open only in case of emergency." But perhaps Jesus understood that if we attach ourselves too firmly to who we *think* Jesus was, then that will make us less inclined to go out in search of the real thing. Being attached to the Jesus of our imagination, we might lack the necessary motivation to venture out in the world to see the many places where the resurrected Christ is still very much among us. Should we remain in one place too long, we risk forgetting Christ's gracious invitation to, "Come and see." [Jn. 1:39]

Therefore, it's somewhat ironic that nowhere else in the world is our human inability to let go is better or more often exhibited than in the church. We cling to doctrine, we cling to dogma, we cling to tradition and habit. We cling to church pews and seating arrangements, portraits of blonde-haired, blue-eyed Jesuses, stained glass, decorations, vestments and robes. We become attached to roles, pastors, committee assignments and to faded, bygone memories of what once was. And for all of these many attachments, we express a certain reluctance to welcome new people into the fold, because newness breeds unfamiliarity; newness brings change. And the last thing we want is to risk this refuge that we have created for ourselves by transforming it into something we can no longer recognize.

But the church was never intended to be a refuge away from the world. The church is not walls or stained glass, or vestments or decoration. Don't get me wrong, the building is nice, (and we here consider ourselves particularly blessed) but we must constantly remind ourselves that the church...the *true* church...is the body of Christ. It is not a building of brick and mortar, but a living and breathing presence out in the world. This structure in which we gather is merely a home and a shelter—a place where this body can rest to gather strength and nourishment for the hard and difficult work to which we have been called—tasks which cannot be accomplished any other place than outside these very walls.

Easter is the time when we celebrate the body of Jesus Christ being raised to new life, both the actual living Christ in the flesh, as well as the collective ability of the faithful to work together and welcome all in his name. And even though we have a human tendency to cling ever so tightly to our personal version of Jesus—even though we have a habit of trying to squeeze the grace of Christ into a tiny little box—an empty tomb testifies to the world that Jesus Christ does not fit so neatly. The grace and peace of Christ has escaped its confines and is running loose in the world once again. As Christ's disciples, nourished through the sacraments and empowered by the Holy Spirit, we boldly venture out to discover where Christ is present and at work in the world. We find Christ present and in the flesh through the love that we share in simple acts of compassion, mercy and forgiveness that each of us experience every day. This is the promise of Resurrection.

Just, try not to get too attached…

Blessing and glory and wisdom and thanksgiving and honor and power and might be to our God forever and ever. Amen.

Themes of freedom and slavery run throughout the whole of scripture. These themes resonate with a child of the American South, who must wrestle mightily with God's demands for justice, when weighed against the sins of his ancestors. It is undeniable that the legacy of slavery continues to have adverse effects upon our society today. It is morally wrong to deny those effects, or to excuse involuntary servitude as somehow "normal" for a particular time or culture. Let us be clear: Slavery is wrong now, just as it was wrong then. Although the writers of the Old and New Testaments avoid addressing institutionalized slavery directly (the Apostle Paul perhaps comes closest in his Letter to Philemon), it is made abundantly clear that the Word of the Lord demands freedom for all God's people; and this means freedom for the whole person— not just a spiritual freedom, and not just a physical freedom. This includes freedom of conscience, freedom from fear, as well as freedom from want and need. The Book of Acts takes us on a journey throughout a culture which was hostile to human freedom, where one's dignity and worth could be bought and sold upon a whim. Paul and the Apostles are beset with the challenge of proclaiming freedom in Jesus Christ to a social, political and economic system which reaps immense profits from the subjugation of others. As much as we like to think human beings have evolved in the course of two thousand years, such abuses remain commonplace. The Gospel speaks loudly on behalf of those in the world who are dragged in chains before the market-place and denied their rightful voice. God has created us to be servants of the divine will, therefore, if we are not serving God, then who or what are we serving?

You Break It, You Buy It

16 One day, as we were going to the place of prayer, we met a slave-girl who had a spirit of divination and brought her owners a great deal of money by fortunetelling. [17]While she followed Paul and us, she would cry out, 'These men are slaves of the Most High God, who proclaim to you a way of salvation.' [18]She kept doing this for many days. But Paul, very much annoyed, turned and said to the spirit, 'I order you in the name of Jesus Christ to come out of her.' And it came out that very hour.

19 But when her owners saw that their hope of making money was gone, they seized Paul and Silas and dragged them into the market-place before the authorities. [20]When they had brought them before the magistrates, they said, 'These men are disturbing our city; they are Jews [21]and are advocating customs that are not lawful for us as Romans to adopt or observe.' [22]The crowd joined in attacking them, and the magistrates had them stripped of their clothing and ordered them to be beaten with

> rods. ²³*After they had given them a severe flogging, they threw them into prison and ordered the jailer to keep them securely. ²⁴Following these instructions, he put them in the innermost cell and fastened their feet in the stocks.*
>
> *25 About midnight Paul and Silas were praying and singing hymns to God, and the prisoners were listening to them. ²⁶Suddenly there was an earthquake, so violent that the foundations of the prison were shaken; and immediately all the doors were opened and everyone's chains were unfastened. ²⁷When the jailer woke up and saw the prison doors wide open, he drew his sword and was about to kill himself, since he supposed that the prisoners had escaped. ²⁸But Paul shouted in a loud voice, 'Do not harm yourself, for we are all here.' ²⁹The jailer called for lights, and rushing in, he fell down trembling before Paul and Silas. ³⁰Then he brought them outside and said, 'Sirs, what must I do to be saved?' ³¹They answered, 'Believe on the Lord Jesus, and you will be saved, you and your household.' ³²They spoke the word of the Lord to him and to all who were in his house. ³³At the same hour of the night he took them and washed their wounds; then he and his entire family were baptized without delay. ³⁴He brought them up into the house and set food before them; and he and his entire household rejoiced that he had become a believer in God.*
>
> Acts 16:16-34 (NRSV)

When we last left our heroes, Paul and Silas, they had just endured a long and grueling 1200mile voyage from Antioch across the Eastern Mediterranean. Along with fellow disciple Timothy, they traveled the length of Asia Minor to the eastern bank of the Bosporus Strait (which would be the western coast of modern-day Turkey). After already going to such tremendous lengths, it was there that Paul received a vision to venture even further across the Aegean Sea, all the way to the city of Philippi in Macedonia, far beyond anywhere Paul had journeyed thus far. Once there, the Spirit directs them to a woman by the name of Lydia, who receives the Good News as she and her household are baptized in Christ's name. This unlikely and improbable encounter is only made possible by the apostles' rugged determination and Lydia's openness of heart, and as a consequence of their mutual effort, the Christian faith gains yet another foothold in foreign soil. In gratitude, Lydia then extends hospitality to the apostles to remain with her in Philippi for some time.

This is where our story picks back up. While in Philippi, Paul and Silas are going about their business when they are confronted by a slave-girl in the marketplace of the city. As the story informs us, this girl is possessed by a spirit of divination, and she made considerable money for her owners by telling the fortunes of others. However, when she comes across Paul and Silas, she accosts them, shouting, *"These men are slaves of the Most High God…"*

This apparently goes on for several days, where Paul and Silas could not even go into the city without this girl going out to confront them, shouting the same thing over and over and over, *"These men are slaves of the Most High God…"* Finally, Paul, losing all patience, turns to the girls and commands the spirit, *"'I order you in the name of Jesus Christ to come out of her!'"* And it does.

Themes of freedom and slavery take center stage in our story as we play witness to these events from the Book of Acts. This girl who is enslaved both in mind and body confronts Paul and Silas and ironically accuses them of being slaves. (Takes one to know one, I suppose.) Yet after Paul frees her of her affliction—after Paul liberates her mind—it is actually the *apostles* who find themselves in chains! In a strange twist of events, Paul and Silas are handed over to the magistrate and thrown into jail. However, while there, a dramatic scene unfolds as the earth begins to tremble as the tools of their imprisonment are broken. Perhaps even stranger, Paul and Silas refuse to escape, but instead use the opportunity to rescue the jailer from a humiliating death and bring his entire household to Christ.

What is freedom? What does it mean to be a slave? These are the questions which this episode from Acts forces us to confront. Such questions have a peculiar relevance for us today. After all, we talk a lot about freedom in this country. It is one of those sacred ideals that Americans hold with such reverence and fervor, and rightfully so. Ever since our very foundation, freedom has been the driving force of our national conversation. We make so much of our freedom of speech, freedom of the press, freedom of choice, freedom of assembly, freedom of this, freedom of that; differing philosophies of freedom continue to shape who we are and how we as a nation perceive ourselves relative to the world around us. Ideals of freedom shape our economy, our politics, our foreign and domestic policy, even our religious faith.

As Americans, we pride ourselves in being a free people, but the question remains: Free to do what? We have all of these freedoms which we believe have been divinely appointed to us by Almighty God, but what do we actually do with them? The most immediate answer always seems to be, "Well…freedom means that I can do whatever I want"—which, quite honestly, is a revealing answer in itself. "Whatever I want…" This sacred ideal of freedom becomes twisted into our excuse for doing what we want to do, rather than what we should do. Oh, we love to cry aloud and yammer on and on when we feel as if our freedom is the least bit threatened, while very little mention is made of the obligations that we owe one another and our God.

"Whatever I want…" You see, we think this makes us free, but when we do what we want to do, rather than what God wants us to do, we merely find our minds and our bodies enslaved to our pettiness and imprisoned by self-serving pride. This conceit and selfishness lead us to the delusion that freedom means that our personal interests come first, the freedom of the community is irrelevant and that the sufferings of others are somehow justified as long as we can get what's ours. As we like to say, "freedom isn't free"—and this is certainly true—but all too often we are content to allow others to pay that price for us. Americans prove all too eager to look past the exploitation of foreign labor, the destruction of communities, the oppression of women and minorities and the pollution and defilement of God's creation, all in the name of profit.

You might think that people would have changed in two-thousand years, but this just comes to show that we really haven't come all that far. After Paul heals the slave-girl, her owners become furious. They vainly exploited this girl's suffering, as long as they could profit from it. Now that Paul has taken away their meal-ticket, they drag him and Silas before the magistrate to level charges against them. But if you will notice, they don't accuse them by saying, "Hey, these guys healed the slave-girl who we were exploiting for profit." No, no…you can't get any moral traction that way. Instead, they say, *"These men are disturbing* **our** *city; they are* **Jews** *and are advocating customs that are not lawful for* **us as Romans** *to adopt or observe."* These *Jews*…these *foreigners*…are causing trouble with their outlandish beliefs and threatening our traditional values. It's the classic "bait and switch", when someone says one thing, but actually mean something else. And like the scoundrels they are, they shallowly invoke patriotism and religious faith to get what they want. They not only appeal to, but *rely* upon others' xenophobia, bigotry and intolerance when accusing the apostles. In other words, these slaveowners reveal themselves to be slaves to hatred, fear and ignorance—the Holy Trinity of Injustice—all summed up on one accusatory statement!

Paul and Silas have come to a foreign land to proclaim freedom in the name of Jesus Christ, and because of this, their freedom is taken away. And why, you ask? Because selfish people foolishly assume that freedom—true freedom and dignity—is somehow bad for business. As a consequence, Paul and Silas are severely beaten and stripped naked by the mob, shackled and thrown into prison, just as Jesus told his servants they would be [Mark 13:9-10]. However, just as the previous scene forces us to reconsider what freedom is, so too does the next compel us to reevaluate what it means to be in bondage. In spite of their present misfortune, Paul and Silas still sing praises and give thanks to God which echoes out from the confines of their prison cell. Even though their bodies are shackled, the apostles remain free to love and serve the Lord. Through Christ, their minds are free, their spirits are free, and because they persevere in faith, this spiritual freedom which they enjoy is dramatically transformed into physical freedom, as the very earth trembles and the power of the Lord swings wide every prison door and shatters every chain.

As the final scene unfolds, the jailer arrives to see what has happened, and fearing that he might be held responsible, he prepares kill himself by falling upon his sword. And yet from the darkness, he hears a voice calling to him forward as Paul and Silas are curiously still there. The apostles do indeed remain in their cells, but they do so as free men, assuming their place among the suffering and the persecuted so that others may be brought to the same freedom which they already know. They show how the Lord's invitation of gracious mercy is extended, not only to the oppressed, but to the oppressor as well, where they too may repent from sin and liberate themselves from being slaves to selfishness and corruption. Confronted with this realization, the jailer takes Paul and Silas into his home and treats the wounds which each had received. He then has his entire family baptized and has a feast prepared for the apostles. And so, this scene that once began with such inhumanity and brutality now ends with fellowship and celebration as former adversaries become reconciled through Jesus Christ. Such is the transformative power of the Good News.

Largely due to his experiences in cities like Philippi, the apostle Paul makes extensive references to freedom and slavery in his own letters. In fact, one could almost construct an entirely new letter based upon those references alone. *"Now the Lord is the Spirit, and where the Spirit of the Lord is, there is freedom."* [2 Cor. 3:17] *"Do you not know that if you present yourselves to anyone as obedient slaves, you are slaves of the one whom you obey, either of sin, which leads to death, or of obedience, which leads to righteousness?"* [Rom. 6:16] *"For freedom Christ has set us free. Stand firm, therefore, and do not submit again to a yoke of slavery."* [Gal. 5:1] *"For you were called to freedom, brothers and sisters; only do not use your freedom as an opportunity for self-indulgence, but through love become slaves to one another. For the whole law is summed up in a single commandment, 'You shall love your neighbor as yourself.'"* [Gal. 5:13-14] *"And that you, having been set free from sin, have become slaves of righteousness."* [Rom. 6:18] *"That is my gospel, for which I suffer hardship, even to the point of being chained like a criminal. But the Word of God is not chained."* [2 Tim. 1:9]

According to Paul, the freedom we enjoy is not some cosmic accident, nor is it something that human beings dreamed up for ourselves, rather freedom is a gift imbued with divine purpose and right intention. For you (yes, you) have been set free to from chains of sin and death to go forth and serve the Lord. (At least in that sense, the slave-girl's fortune has indeed come true, as that is the destiny for all Christians to be servants of the Most High God.) Since you have received true freedom in Jesus Christ, what will you do with it? Will you remain bound by sinfulness and self-indulgence, or will you instead serve the will of the Lord who purchased your redemption, that you may become the person who God has created you to be? In freedom, we are called to free others—to free the mind from ignorance and complacency, free the spirit from fear and hopelessness, and to free the body from want and need. Your chains have been broken. You also have been bought with a price—a price that someone else was willing to pay because he believed that you were worth it. Now the question remains: Are you?

Blessing and glory and wisdom and thanksgiving and honor and power and might be to our God forever and ever. Amen.

Like many pastors, every now and again, I will lead a vespers service at a local retirement community for folks in assisted living. It's always a delicate situation when one preaches, "do justice, love kindness and walk humbly with your God" to persons with significant mobility and health concerns, who can no longer, "go and do" as they once could. I try to encourage such persons with messages which emphasize the power of prayer, since prayer itself can be a transformative act. Prayer was an essential element of Jesus' own ministry, a means by which he empowered himself for the hard and difficult work of serving God. Prayer is an act of resistance against people or things which seek to supplant God's claim over our lives. Prayer encourages us and reorients us by providing the necessary focus so that we might see God's presence in the world with greater clarity. Pastors are truly blessed in the sense that we often bear witness to the power of prayer first-hand, both in the one who prays and ones being prayed for. But even so, given our demanding work schedules along with life's many obligations, sometimes we too forget to pray as we should. Therefore, I wrote this sermon as a reminder, not only for the church, but also for myself, that sometimes to follow where Christ leads, one has to stop and be still—for a change.

Famous Last Words

1 After Jesus had spoken these words, he looked up to heaven and said, 'Father, the hour has come; glorify your Son so that the Son may glorify you, ²since you have given him authority over all people, to give eternal life to all whom you have given him. ³And this is eternal life, that they may know you, the only true God, and Jesus Christ whom you have sent. ⁴I glorified you on earth by finishing the work that you gave me to do. ⁵So now, Father, glorify me in your own presence with the glory that I had in your presence before the world existed.

6 'I have made your name known to those whom you gave me from the world. They were yours, and you gave them to me, and they have kept your word. ⁷Now they know that everything you have given me is from you; ⁸for the words that you gave to me I have given to them, and they have received them and know in truth that I came from you; and they have believed that you sent me. ⁹I am asking on their behalf; I am not asking on behalf of the world, but on behalf of those whom you gave me, because they are yours. ¹⁰All mine are yours, and yours are mine; and I have been glorified in them. ¹¹And now I am no longer in the world, but they are in the world, and I am coming to you. Holy Father, protect them in your name that you have given me, so that they may be one, as we are one.

John 17:1-11 (NRSV)

I hate tour groups. I suppose they're okay for some, just not for me. I gotta be free, man…I have to roam. That's just how *I* roll. After all, try squeezing 6' 5" of "Grade A" expatriate North Carolinian into a cramped tour bus seat for hours and hours on end every day; add to this volatile mixture several annoying tour guides, some mild dehydration, a general lack of sleep and a pinch of tourist fatigue, shake lightly and what you get is one unhappy camper. On the tour bus, you spend so much time with the same three dozen or so people being constantly herded from one destination to the next that it makes it quite difficult for even this self-proclaimed disciple of Saint Arthur Fonzarelli of Milwaukee to retain his cool.

So, you can probably imagine my state of mind fifteen days into my seminary's Middle East travel seminar as our tour bus pulled up outside the Church of All Nations in Jerusalem. The Church of all Nations is a modest sized basilica built by the Roman Catholics at the foot of the Mount of Olives to commemorate the traditional spot of Christ's betrayal and arrest. And I must say that despite my mood at the time, it was a beautiful church. Corinthian marble columns gracefully support archways of gold leaf as beautiful tile mosaics adorn the walls. Sparse windows of purple stained glass add a certain dignity to the dimly lit sanctuary as a modest assembly of Catholic priests led mass before a patch of exposed earth where it is believed Jesus knelt to pray, *'Abba, Father, for you all things are possible; remove this cup from me; yet, not what I want, but what you want.'* [Mk. 14:36] Surrounding this church were the legendary gardens of Gethsemane itself, with meticulously landscaped beds of roses and ancient olive trees filling the cloister with the quiet rustle of leaves and bird feathers amid the dry desert air.

But after two weeks, I had just about enough of traveling, tour groups, a severe lack of legroom, tourist traps, motion sickness, estimated travel times, exchange rates, and fellow seminarians with comments so *ridiculous* it made me just want to punch someone in the face! All in all, I was in no mood to be moved, and these distractions made it nearly impossible to make any connection between the Gardens of Gethsemane from the Bible and the one that lay before my very eyes. What should have served as solemn reminder of Christ's sacrifice for humankind became reduced to little more than another obstacle on my holy pilgrimage to the hotel bar.

But believe it or not, in retrospect, I am very glad that my wife and I went on this travel seminar. This was really the first of many such adventures that we've shared in our lives together. We saw lands and places that we might have never gotten a chance to see otherwise. We felt the cool desert evening air on our faces as the sun set from the Mount of Olives, and ran the azure waters of the Sea of Galilee between our fingers. We got to crawl through the pyramids of Egypt and hear the morning call to prayer amid the rooftops of Amman. We got to witness the harsh an unforgiving terrain of the Sinai wilderness and float feet forward upon the surface of the Dead Sea. These experiences gave physical form to these lands that prior had existed only in my imagination, and I know that I am a better pastor for having gone there to witness these things first hand.

I guess what bothers me about my time in Gethsemane was that I let it all get to me. I allowed the world to intrude. I came away disappointed with myself that I allowed the stresses and strains of traveling distract me from experiencing what many consider to be one of the holiest sites in Christendom.

However, I do take some solace in that fact that I was not alone. The Gardens of Gethsemane have known their fair share of chaos and distraction. Whenever I read these preceding chapters from the Gospel of John, I picture a whirlwind scene as Jesus embarks from the Last Supper full of commotion, frantically leading his disciples through the winding streets of Jerusalem on the way to meet his reward. As the disciples struggle to keep pace with him, Jesus continues to bark out last-second instructions to them, how they should love one another and faithfully face the hatred of the world with that very same love. Jesus talks in cryptic metaphors describing vines and vine keepers, fire, emotion and the birth pangs of new life. He speaks to the disciples of advocates, new commandments, betrayals and denials yet to come, taking every opportunity to squeeze in just one more lesson for their instruction and benefit.

And I suppose this reveals the true difference between Jesus and myself. Even as Jesus is dealing with these many distractions, as we reach the seventeenth chapter of John's gospel, the tone of the scene instantly changes from frantic to almost tranquil. Even though he faces the prospect of an untimely and violent death upon the cross, once Jesus enters the Garden, he becomes strangely at peace. Looking up to heaven, he prays aloud, "*Father, the hour has come; glorify your Son so that the Son may glorify you…*" Unlike other instances in the gospels when Jesus goes off by himself to pray alone, this time he invites his disciples around him that we may bear witness to how life with God should be: Open and vulnerable, humble and serene, wholly trusting in God's steadfast love. Perhaps it's no accident that this is the final lesson that Jesus has for his disciples.

The scene that unfolds at Gethsemane is rendered more poignant when we realize for what and for whom Jesus is praying. He prays to the Father, *"I am asking on their behalf; I am not asking on behalf of the world, but on behalf of those whom you gave me, because they are yours. All mine are yours, and yours are mine; and I have been glorified in them. And now I am no longer in the world, but they are in the world, and I am coming to you. Holy Father, protect them in your name that you have given me, so that they may be one, as we are one."*

With all of the perils that Jesus now faces, with all that must weigh heavily upon his overburdened mind, as armed soldiers in the distance make their way through the olive groves, while the torches in their hands begin to cast a faint glow upon his cheek, Jesus' last act as a free man is to pray for his disciples. He prays for us, so that we may share in his glory. The distractions, the chaos and the dangers of an uncertain future are all still very much present, and with the echoes of iron chains ringing in the darkness, though his humble act of prayer and supplication there is a sense of perfect freedom as Jesus immediately puts all of these mortal concerns into their proper place by placing them into the hands of God.

We forget that…we forget there is *freedom* in the act of prayer. Too often we are reluctant to pray because our egos see prayer strictly as an act of submission, but we must bear in mind that it is an act of submission to a sovereign God to whom all other concerns give sway. Through prayer we are liberated from those things that distract us from living a life of faith; it is a means of quieting all of those competing voices in our heads that we might listen for the voice of God more clearly. No matter whether we are at home, or half a world away—it doesn't matter if we are held captive by our problems or by disability—it is the act of prayer which will forever empower us. And maybe we can't find the right words, and maybe we don't know exactly what we should be praying for, but God refuses to hold such things against us. No matter what—no matter what trials we face in this life, no matter our state of mind or the condition of our body—it doesn't matter how smart we are, it doesn't matter how strong we are—we *always* have the power to pray for ourselves and for others. Prayer is the one refuge in the mind that no mortal concern can ever touch, and we take great heart knowing that someone out there is listening.

When our group of intrepid world travelers got back from the Middle East about this time of year (I guess *ten* years ago! Yikes!), this was the passage that was waiting for me in the lectionary upon my return to my church internship that following Sunday. Perhaps ironically, or (who knows?) perhaps intentionally, fate had one last lesson for me to glean there as well—a lesson to, "take time to smell the roses" in the Garden of Gethsemane, to find the time and the discipline to pray to God and to place the distractions of a mortal life in their proper perspective so that I, too might behold the glory of the Lord. And I will admit that I have yet to get it right. After all, life is hard…prayer is hard. But I take comfort in the knowledge that there is someone out there who is praying for us with a love that makes all things possible—a love strong enough to unite us all as one.

Blessing and glory and wisdom and thanksgiving and honor and power and might be to our God forever and ever. Amen.

The Paul of Galatians may be my favorite representation of the apostle. We understand from the outset how the apostle is in full-on offensive mode, going after critics who have sought to displace him as an authority within Christ's church. Raw emotion and religious zeal come boiling to the surface in unexpected ways. ("I wish those who unsettle you would castrate themselves!" he boldly states in 5:12...The Word of the Lord, indeed!) Too often, people imagine the people of the Bible as spiritually detached from our human experience, but nothing could be further from hot-blooded, passionate truth. Apostles, patriarchs and prophets, even Jesus himself, possessed the full range of joys and frustrations which are commonplace in the exercise of their calling. The Letter to the Galatians drives that home for us in glorious detail.

This sermon was delivered on a day when our congregation welcomed an openly gay man into our congregation through the sacrament of baptism, something which would have been unthinkable under the previous leadership. He and his husband arrived at our church and have remained because of the welcome they received—not a false welcome, or a conditional welcome, but and genuine appreciation of having them as part of our faith community. In First Waynesboro, they discovered a place where they could worship the Lord with honestly and sincerity, celebrating who they are and the love they share. We often take for granted the simple pleasures of sitting beside our spouse in the pews, or singing from the same hymnal, but these two were experiencing such blessings for the first time! And because of the extent to which they and other LGBTQ persons have embraced life within our faith community, this has affirmed First Waynesboro's decision to persevere in unity with our denomination as the correct one. Moreover, our experience has demonstrated that churches and leaders who proclaim doctrines of exclusion are fundamentally wrong in their understanding of the gospel. Only recognition of our shared brokenness can provide the humility necessary to accept others without qualification. This isn't a popularity contest; it's about doing what is right.

Direct from the Source

1 Paul an apostle—sent neither by human commission nor from human authorities, but through Jesus Christ and God the Father, who raised him from the dead— ²and all the members of God's family who are with me,

To the churches of Galatia:

3 Grace to you and peace from God our Father and the Lord Jesus Christ,[4]who gave himself for our sins to set us free from the present evil age, according to the will of our God and Father, [5]to whom be the glory for ever and ever. Amen.

6 I am astonished that you are so quickly deserting the one who called you in the grace of Christ and are turning to a different gospel— [7]not that there is another gospel, but there are some who are confusing you and want to pervert the gospel of Christ. [8]But even if we or an angel from heaven should proclaim to you a gospel contrary to what we proclaimed to you, let that one be accursed! [9]As we have said before, so now I repeat, if anyone proclaims to you a gospel contrary to what you received, let that one be accursed!

10 Am I now seeking human approval, or God's approval? Or am I trying to please people? If I were still pleasing people, I would not be a servant of Christ.

11 For I want you to know, brothers and sisters, that the gospel that was proclaimed by me is not of human origin; [12]for I did not receive it from a human source, nor was I taught it, but I received it through a revelation of Jesus Christ.

Galatians 1:1-12 (NRSV)

For our scripture lesson this week we once again return to words written by the hand the Apostle Paul. Now, as I've mentioned to you before, Paul's writings lie at the heart of our understanding of the Christian faith. One might think of him as first and foremost among the theologians. His apostolic missions were critical to the formation of the early church, and church communities often appealed to Paul as the highest of authorities. The ancient church revered his teachings and his ministry to such a degree that his words are not simply regarded as treatise or commentary, but as *scripture* which stand on equal par with the Old Testament, the Ten Commandments and even the gospels themselves! Indeed, early compilations of Paul's letters, written many years before the gospels, very likely formed the foundation of what would eventually evolve into the New Testament!

But the person of Paul is not without controversy. Sometimes, when you mention his name among pastors and professors, there is no shortage of eyerolling that goes on. Many of his articulated beliefs on sin, justification, idolatry, the role of women in the church, the relation of the gospel to Jewish tradition, continue to be the source of debate and speculation. This is further complicated by all the writers after Paul who produced letters and texts in his name during the decades following his death, or perhaps edited existing letters to address issues present in the church during their own time. As such, we are not entirely sure of who Paul actually was, and separating man from myth can prove quite challenging. Of the thirteen letters attributed to Paul in the New Testament, only seven are believed to have been definitively written by Paul's hand. That's all…seven letters. Imagine if you only had a handful of pages to tell the church and the world who you are and what you believe!

Paul can be controversial nowadays, but as we learned in our recent bible study on First and Second Corinthians, Paul was a controversial figure even in his own time. Again and again, Paul was forced to defend his teachings and sometime even his character before a barrage of criticisms leveled against him. Yet of all the many criticisms which Paul faced in his lifetime, the one which seemed to have dogged him the most was the question of his authority. Even then, people often wondered, how did Paul gain such distinction as a Christian leader? Establishing one's credentials was a common practice in the teaching life of the early church. As was the custom of the day, one had to be able to trace one's learning back through a particular disciple to Christ himself. Incidentally, that is why we have four gospels named for the apostles Matthew, Mark, Luke and John. Each one sought to attribute their teaching back to the source through a particular school of thought. These credentials are what provided one with, what we call, "apostolic authority".

And for all Paul's passion and for all Paul's intellect, this was the one area in which he was lacking. Paul was not one of the original twelve disciples, nor was he was not one of the seventy commissioned by Jesus from Luke, and for all we know, he never actually met Christ in the flesh. As a man who originated from Tarsus in Asia Minor hundreds of miles away, he was not associated with the movement in Galilee in any way; in fact, Paul earned a rather suspicious reputation as a persecutor of the early church. The only connection Paul ever shared with Christ was this mysterious and sudden conversion which inexplicably brought him to the Christian cause. But nevertheless, in spite of his many successes founding and strengthening congregations throughout the Mediterranean world, many of Paul's opponents were aware of his dubious apostolic credentials, and apparently, he was reminded quite frequently of that very fact.

For this reason, the letter to the Galatians begins on a somewhat defensive note. From the very first words of the very first line of the epistle, Paul identifies himself in no uncertain terms to his audience, *"Paul an* **apostle**—*sent neither by human commission nor from human authorities, but through Jesus Christ and God the Father."* A few lines later he underscores this again, *"For I want you to know, brothers and sisters, that the gospel that was proclaimed by me is not of human origin; for I did not receive it from a human source, nor was I taught it, but I received it through a revelation of Jesus Christ."*

As we were wrapping up our study on First and Second Corinthians, I spent a moment reflecting on how one is called to the ministry. When you go off to seminary, there will come a time when you will inevitably find yourself sitting in a circle with a bunch of strangers—in a small group, social gathering or whatnot—and someone will ask you to share your "call story". What essentially led you to pursue a theological education and perhaps become a pastor? Now even at this early point in the process, you've shared this story a few dozen times already, with various committees, interviews, etc., and even though it's starting to become a running joke, this is still something everyone wants to know, and you will even have to tell it a couple hundred more times as you move through the ordination process!

But nevertheless, as these individual stories make their way around the circle, you quickly realize how unique each person's sense of call truly is. You have people like me, who had to take a long time to realize their sense of call, and you had others who knew they wanted to be a pastor since they were children. You had people who were carrying on a family legacy into the third or fourth generation of pastors, and you even had those who truly believe that the very hand of God had reached down to touch their tongue that they might proclaim the gospel!

Needless to say, there could be quite a disconnect between these various experiences, and one may easily regard another with a certain degree of suspicion. As someone who struggled mightily with my own sense of call, I found it very difficult to relate to those who suddenly felt "chosen", and they in all likelihood felt the same way about me. But I would eventually discover there is no singular method by which one is called. Each of us is unique, and yet it took a certain amount of maturity on my part to finally recognize how God calls different people in a multitude of ways. And whether we realized that sense of call suddenly, or gradually over time, we affirm that it all comes from the same source which lies outside of ourselves. Apostolic truth has origins in the divine. It is the Lord who calls, it is the Lord who ordains, it is the Lord who sets aside those to serve God's purpose.

Now, we consider ourselves to be what Martin Luther famously referred to as, "the Priesthood of All Believers." That is, we have each been called according to our individual gifts (given to us by the Holy Spirit) in the service of God, and no particular set of gifts is more valuable than those of another. At least in that sense, we are all called to be leaders in the church, whether as clergy or as laypeople. What we believe as a church is often shaped by the particular challenges we are presently facing, therefore time and circumstance have much to do with who is called to be a leader in the church and why. However, at the same time, it is equally important to remember that it does not matter how confident one may be in their sense of call—it does not matter how good one is a public-speaking, theological knowledge, biblical interpretation or even speaking in tongues—no one gets to be a leader in the church simply because they want to be! It is only the Holy Spirit working through the community of the faithful who ultimately validates that sense of call.

So, it was for Paul. Despite the criticism, he faced in his lifetime, it was ultimately the community who vindicated the truth of his words. Not only did Paul's correspondence affirm what the early church believed as a community, but also expressed who they felt God was calling them to be! As we can all attest, then as with now, there is no shortage of self-appointed apostles in the world. There are those who preach a self-important gospel that will tell you with 100% certainty who is saved and who is damned, who is righteous and who is a sinner. There are those who advance narrow ideology in the guise of religion, or sell salvation to the highest bidder. There are those who abuse the Word of God to justify their contempt for those different than themselves. But such narrowmindedness has never been part of our Christian tradition. Messages grounded in hatred, ignorance and exclusion run contrary to the gospel which we have received, and in time, such words will be revealed for what they truly are, as well as the source from whence they came.

Ours, by comparison, is a message of irresistible grace and unconditional love, and the peace which such knowledge provides. That is who we are, and God willing, who we hope to be. Paul is certainly known for some tough talk, but if you will notice, every single one of Paul's letters (including the one to the

Galatians) begins by wishing those in Christ's church grace and peace, as grace and peace provide the context for every word which is to follow.

Baptism is the perfect opportunity for taking stock of ourselves as individuals and as a church to examine the many ways in which God is working through us as apostles of the Good News. Through the presence of the Holy Spirit, we come to understand how we have been each touched by the life-giving waters of God's grace, and how we have been called by our Lord to share that grace with others. If we are intent on existing as a truly welcoming community, then there will no doubt be many in the world who will not approve of such openness, but it is not our calling to seek their approval; we only seek the approval of the One who goes to incredible lengths to welcome each of God's children into the presence of the divine.

Blessing and glory and wisdom and thanksgiving and honor and power and might be to our God forever and ever. Amen.

If we are to take seriously God's promises of redemption and new life, then we must take into account how they apply to the whole of our lives, not just our individual mortality. Our collective life in the church is a prime example. You may notice how congregations and individual people share much in common, as each possesses a unique personality all their own. And when confronted with a particular challenge, they respond in different ways. Obviously most, if not all, congregations are keenly aware of national trends which show a consistent decline in membership and participation within the American church. Some of these congregations have responded to these challenges in healthy ways by strengthening community, while others have responded in not-so-healthy ways, placing growth or ideology above mission. In spite of the uncertainty, the 21st century represents a valuable opportunity for congregations and denominations to reexamine why they are a church and how God has called them to serve, for above all else, we must be the church of our time and place— nothing more, nothing less. It's quite clear that the church is not the same as it was just a few short decades ago. Like any living and breathing entity, the church should always be evolving and adapting to new environments.

It's plausible that whatever emerges from these changes will seem unrecognizable to us today. Sure, this may be a time of great anxiety, but it is also a time of great hope. I for one, look forward to seeing what the future holds.

Déjà Vu All Over Again

11 Soon afterwards Jesus went to a town called Nain, and his disciples and a large crowd went with him. ^{12}As he approached the gate of the town, a man who had died was being carried out. He was his mother's only son, and she was a widow; and with her was a large crowd from the town.^{13}When the Lord saw her, he had compassion for her and said to her, 'Do not weep.' ^{14}Then he came forward and touched the bier, and the bearers stood still. And he said, 'Young man, I say to you, rise!' ^{15}The dead man sat up and began to speak, and Jesus gave him to his mother. ^{16}Fear seized all of them; and they glorified God, saying, 'A great prophet has risen among us!' and 'God has looked favorably on his people!' ^{17}This word about him spread throughout Judea and all the surrounding country.

Luke 7:11-17 (NRSV)

When we come upon Jesus in the eleventh chapter of the Gospel of Luke, we bear witness to a tale which seems strikingly familiar. Those reading this passage immediately recognize strong parallels between this story and a similar tale from the book of First Kings from the Old Testament—another faraway town, another widow, another deceased son, another man of God come to save the day. Both stories begin with the same set of circumstances and both stories conclude with the same result, as the one sent from God rescues the son from life to death, thus restoring the hope of the widow mother. Both stories testify to the power of the Lord, and show those gathered around that the Lord is not a God of death, but a God of life.

The people in our story from Luke see what Jesus does before them and behold him as the new Elijah. *"A great prophet has risen among us!"* they shout. And with a comparison such as that, Jesus finds himself in some rather exclusive company. After all, Elijah wasn't just "a" prophet, he was "the" prophet, perhaps second only in stature to Moses himself! Elijah was the one who single-handedly frustrated the plans of Queen Jezebel and her priests of Baal. Elijah was the one who summoned fire from the sky and spoke with angels. Elijah was the one who stood in the very presence of God and lived to tell the tale. In time, a flaming chariot would carry Elijah to the heavens, whereby the people of God would await his arrival to herald the coming the Messiah on the Day of the Lord. And so, by performing the very same miracle which Elijah did, many of these long-awaiting people must have wondered: Could this *finally* be him?

It's undeniable that this episode of Jesus from Luke's gospel shares much in common with the one of Elijah from First Kings, but the truth of the story is not revealed in the similarities, but the differences. If we compare the passages, First Kings requires a long set-up by the tale which precedes it. Luke, by contrast, presents the passage as almost an afterthought. Elijah acts in response to accusations by the widow, whereas Jesus takes initiative to act on his own. It takes Elijah praying over the boy three times to achieve the desired result, yet Jesus only must speak once. Elijah stretches himself, physically pressing himself upon the body of the son, but Jesus merely touches the stand upon which the body lies. And last but perhaps most importantly, Elijah repeatedly cries out to God in loud lamentation, "Why, O Lord my God? Why? Why?" Compare that to Jesus who merely commands the son to rise, "Young man, **I** say to you, rise," and just like that, it happens!

Those assembled persons who witness this miracle and declare, "A great prophet has risen among us", are not entirely incorrect, but by jumping to this conclusion, they kind of miss the point of the miracle. Elijah has received his authority as a prophet from the Lord, and yet Jesus' authority appears to originate from Jesus himself! By showing similarities among these stories, Luke makes it abundantly clear that Jesus is no ordinary prophet, and yet by highlighting the differences between them, it is also revealed that Jesus is no *extraordinary* prophet—clearly, he is much, much more than this. Once upon a time, Elijah heralded the coming rain to restore life to a land suffering from drought, and now with the arrival of Jesus, an entire world in desperate need of redemption may now anticipate a deluge of God's abundant and life-giving grace.

The Lord is not a God of death, but a God of life. This familiar theme is repeated again and again throughout scripture. If we read the bible from cover to cover, the Lord creates life in the beginning and then raises all creation to new life at the end. Life is what the whole story is about. And yet human beings are fixated on death. Fear of dying governs so much of what we do. We possess entire industries designed to protect us from an untimely demise, from medicine to the military, from automobiles to safety-helmets, from door-locks to bath-mats, to those little yellow labels on the stepladder telling you upon which surfaces you should and should not place the darn thing. And don't get me wrong. Life is good, protecting life is good, and wanting to improve the quantity and quality of life is a truly noble pursuit, but the depth of our fear and fixation cause us to regard death as *abnormal*—as something decidedly unnatural. Life is so precious to us, that when people face the very real prospect of dying, they can feel as if they've somehow failed. (And we're not alone; even Jesus himself confessed his own fear of death when he prayed to God for that dreaded cup to pass at Gethsemane. [Mt. 26:39])

As a pastor, you encounter death all the time, but it's never something you get used to. It's just one of those things which comes with the territory, I suppose. You see people in the hospital– people you know, people you care about—as they struggle in their final moments of life. You see them hooked up to all the beeping and whirring machines, surrounded by a vigil of friends and loved ones, with nurses and hospice workers checking in on them in all hours of the night, and they struggle mightily to summon the strength to speak or maintain consciousness for just a minute longer. You see the fear in their eyes as they come to terms with the inevitable truth; yet most often, the fear is not for themselves, rather it is fear for their families and loved ones. They don't want to let them down and are ashamed of their weakness. So, we'll try to assuage those fears by offering platitudes like, "Hope you feel better," when we know that's not going to be the case. And I'll confess that I'm the worst offender when it comes to denying the reality of death. Sometimes, as I leave the hospital room after such a difficult visitation, I'll say something trite like, "I'll check in with you later", or, "I'll see you again soon", which I suppose is not entirely untrue, but it does kind of miss the overall point, and as a result, the opportunity to speak truthfully about death is lost, because quite honestly, I don't want to face it myself.

I've told you before about my friend, colleague and mentor, Carl Tinsley, who pastored one of the local African-American congregations in Buena Vista during my tenure there. While we were preparing for a joint service one day, Carl was talking candidly about his recent diagnosis with terminal lung cancer. He mentioned how many well-intentioned people would see him and tell him how sorry they were that he was sick, but Carl would always reply, "I'm not sick; I just have cancer." And you just couldn't help but admire his outlook. Carl would courageously remind me how death is not unnatural, quite the opposite, it may actually be the most natural thing in the world. God did not create us to live forever, in God's wisdom, that's just how we were made to be, and of all the things Jesus healed people of in the gospels, mortality was not one of them. If death is truly something in which we all have a share, perhaps then we should not regard dying as a failure, but as an opportunity to make the best use of the life we have left!

So, let's broaden things out a bit. Let's focus for moment upon the life of a congregation. What's the worst possible thing one can accuse a church of nowadays? The greatest shame in modern Christianity is to become known as a "dying" church. "Oh, them…they're a *dying* church. Poor them…That congregation is dying." And just as with individuals, that fear of death can end up dictating everything a congregation does. (I've seen it a hundred times) So what do they do? They cut back on mission, they cut back on outreach, they cut back on fellowship and educational opportunities; they circle those proverbial wagons and turn inward trying to squirrel away every last cent. Sometimes, they exist in denial by doubling-down upon extreme ideologies and narrow worldviews in an attempt to prove themselves the fittest and the most worthy of the lot. They'll try to squeeze every last ounce of life they possibly can, but all they ever really do is hasten their own demise. Oh, their quantity of life may increase, but the quality of that life is poor as the vitality of the church becomes slowly drained away. They forget who they are and lose sight of who God has called them to be, all as a consequence of trying to wash themselves from the stench of death and the stigma of alleged failure.

One might even be so bold to claim, by trying so desperately to save their life, they only end up losing it.

I know this may not be a terribly fashionable thing to say in our day and age, but I for one, have decided to embrace the idea of belonging to a dying church. (That's right, I said it *embrace* the idea of belonging to a dying church!) And why? Because when you think about it, all congregations are "dying churches"! Don't get me wrong, God's universal church will live forever, but the earthly church will continue to change and evolve, just as it always has. The church will assume a variety of forms in many new and different places; buildings will go up, doors will close, this church will shrink, that church will grow, but in the end, regardless of what form it assumes, it will still be the church! And no congregation, indeed no denomination, is meant to live forever. Everything that has a beginning, has an end. Mortal institutions meet mortal conclusions—that is simply the nature of life. All congregations are dying—this one, the one across the street, the big one with all the young people and families out in the suburbs, even that 5,000-member megachurch you see on television, in time, they will all disappear from the face of the earth. It may take ten years, it may take twenty, it may take ten-thousand, but they will reach their end nonetheless, just as we all do.

Therefore, Christians everywhere need to rediscover our identity as a dying church. And why? So, we can make the best possible use of the life we have left. Our mission, our outreach, our worship and our fellowship all need to be fixed upon hope and life, not fear and death, because our God is the God of life. In life together—that is where we find God. Acknowledging the *reality* of death—this is not failure, this is not surrender; this is having the vision and the courage to look beyond the mortal veil in anticipation of what is next. Death is not an end, but a new beginning; for only by dying, are we raised to new life by our Lord. Once we accept that fact, then maybe we can finally get around to doing the Lord's business.

If I had a nickel for every self-help book designed to prevent a church from gaining a reputation as a "dying congregation", I would likely be a multimillionaire by now. Countless pastors, professionals and Ph.D.'s reap royalties catering to the mortal anxieties that every single church experiences in this modern age in which we live. Some of their advice can be insightful, others—well, not so much. It's impossible to tell from the cover which is which. So, who then, should you look to? Do you want to truly grow as a church? Then look to Christ. Do you want to increase in faith and fellowship? Look to Christ. Do you want to live as the Body of Christ? If so, then you need to be doing the things that Jesus himself would be doing: loving and serving, giving and forgiving, welcoming and teaching, praying and healing, living, and yes, even *dying*. Take heart and know that we do not go anywhere that Christ has not gone first. When Jesus was facing the prospect of his own death, he never held back anything—not for one moment. He was not ashamed to be seen as weak or vulnerable, and when all was said and done, Jesus did not discover new life until he had offered the world every last thing he had. Maybe there's a lesson for the church in there somewhere…

For no matter if we are talking about congregations or individuals, each life is different. Each person has a story to tell. This is also how God has made us. So, we must consider the question: Are we being true to ourselves? In our Presbyterian *Book of Common Worship*, there's a line from the funeral liturgy which has always resonated with me. It reads, *"Help us to live as those who are prepared to die, and when our days are ended, enable us to die as those who go forth to live, so that living or dying, our life may be in Jesus Christ our risen Lord."*[1] You see, that is our prayer; that is who we are and who we hope to be. In the meantime, we just need to learn how to tell our story. If we look solely to what we share in common with churches of other Christian traditions, that's all well and good, but if that's all we do, we kind of miss the overall point. How much richer, how much more powerful and how much more meaningful will our story be because of those tiny differences, not just the similarities. Our truth will be revealed in the life which sets us apart to show the world how special and unique God has created us to be.

Blessing and glory and wisdom and thanksgiving and honor and power and might be to our God forever and ever. Amen.

1. Presbyterian Church (USA) & the Cumberland Presbyterian Church, *Book of Common Worship*, p. 916, Westminster John Knox Press, 1993

Obviously, 2016 was not a great year for race relations in the United States. By now, we're dreadfully familiar with the frequent headlines which described the death of unarmed black men at the hands of police. What makes matters even more heartbreaking are those in the public sphere who feel it necessary to direct antipathy toward the victim or protestors in the wake of such incidents. Ignorance of the issues forces ordinarily good people into taking sides over ethical considerations which should be beyond all doubt. Killing is wrong, and the killing of defenseless persons is even more wrong! So, how do you awaken your white, suburban upper middle class congregation to the reality of racial injustice when they are socially and economically (even geographically) insulated from it? No doubt words will have little effect upon hardened hearts. But I do know what Martin Luther King, Jr. described as, "the appalling silence" of white Christians will only exacerbate tensions if we refuse to hold people, leaders and institutions to account.

First Presbyterian of Waynesboro has an inconsistent history when it comes to race relations. Following Reconstruction, the church was one of the few in the state of Virginia who conducted integrated worship services. The church supported a black missionary by the name of William P. Sheppard, Jr. (a.k.a., "The Black Livingstone") who served in the Congo in the late 19th century and brought many of the abuses of the Belgian military occupation to light. And yet during the 1960's, this church fired clergy for their participation in the Civil Rights Movement and the March on Washington. As we seek to reclaim our heritage as a welcoming and inclusive institution, we must understand how race needs to be part of that conversation.

I first wrote a draft of this sermon as the city of Baltimore was still smoldering after Freddie Gray died while in police custody in April of 2015. Again, it's one of those sermons that I hoped to never deliver again, but circumstances would dictate otherwise.

All Good Things

26 Then an angel of the Lord said to Philip, 'Get up and go towards the south to the road that goes down from Jerusalem to Gaza.' (This is a wilderness road.) 27So he got up and went. Now there was an Ethiopian eunuch, a court official of the Candace, queen of the Ethiopians, in charge of her entire treasury. He had come to Jerusalem to worship 28and was returning home; seated in his chariot, he was reading the prophet Isaiah. 29Then the Spirit said to Philip, 'Go over to this chariot and join it.' 30So Philip ran up to it and heard him reading the prophet Isaiah. He asked, 'Do you understand what you are reading?' ³¹*He replied, 'How can I, unless someone guides me?' And he invited Philip to get in and sit beside him.* ³²*Now the passage of the scripture that he was reading was this:*

*'Like a sheep, he was
led to the slaughter, and
like a lamb silent before
its shearer, so he does
not open his mouth.*
³³ *In his humiliation justice was denied him.
  Who can describe his generation?
For his life is taken away from the earth.'*

³⁴*The eunuch asked Philip, 'About whom, may I ask you, does the prophet say this, about himself or about someone else?'* ³⁵*Then Philip began to speak, and starting with this scripture, he proclaimed to him the good news about Jesus.* ³⁶*As they were going along the road, they came to some water; and the eunuch said, 'Look, here is water! What is to prevent me from being baptized?'* ³⁸*He commanded the chariot to stop, and both of them, Philip and the eunuch, went down into the water, and Philip baptized him.* ³⁹*When they came up out of the water, the Spirit of the Lord snatched Philip away; the eunuch saw him no more, and went on his way rejoicing.* ⁴⁰*But Philip found himself at Azotus, and as he was passing through the region, he proclaimed the good news to all the towns until he came to Caesarea.*

Acts 8:26-40 (NRSV)

Just before I started at this church last year, Myra and I founds ourselves on vacation in California, and so we decided to leave San Francisco and spend a few days traveling up in Sonoma wine country. In order to do this, we had to find a rental car. After some research, we managed to find a pretty good deal on the internet, and so the next day, we packed up our bags and took the subway to nearby Oakland International Airport to pick up our ride at the rental agency. Before catching our connecting train to the terminal, our train paused ever so briefly at a stop called Fruitvale Station. Fruitvale Station is probably not a place that many folks are familiar with. It is a simple, innocuous train platform rising just above the light posts of Oakland's industrial inner city. The station takes its name from the surrounding neighborhood, which in the 19th century was once cultivated with orchards of cherry and apricot trees. Although we may not know much about the place itself, almost seven years ago there was an incident which has unfortunately become all too familiar: A young, unarmed black man, a white police officer, a gunshot, another life wasted, another community torn asunder.

Owen Grant III was just 22 years old at the time of his death. After celebrating the New Year in San Francisco, Grant was returning home through Fruitvale Station along with some friends when an altercation developed on the subway platform between themselves and another group of young people. Fueled by drugs and alcohol, a fight soon ensued, and a couple of Transit Police Officers quickly arrived on the scene to restore order. The officers seated the suspects against the wall, and as Grant protested his innocence, strong words and insults were exchanged with the officers while they attempted to pin Grant face down to the ground to handcuff him. In the middle of the scuffle, one of the officers unholstered his sidearm. A single gunshot rang out striking Grant in the back, exiting out of his chest, ricocheting off the concrete floor and striking him again, puncturing his lung. Paramedics arrived on the scene in an attempt to stabilize him, yet Grant would die seven hours later at a nearby hospital.

As we have recently seen in other places, in the wake of the killing, the people of Oakland took to the streets in protest. Protests were peaceful for the most part, but many others took advantage of the unrest, ransacking and looting several area businesses, burning cars, throwing rocks and bottles at police officers and causing millions of dollars in damage to the city. The police responded in kind with riot gear, tear gas and a declared curfew. Calls for a federal investigation into the killing were issued, but nothing ever came of it. Eventually things would settle down in Oakland, but the shooting touched off what many had long suspected, that there were severe social and economic divides within the city, divides which now would take considerable time to heal. Yet time would reveal that such divides are not exclusive to Oakland, but they exist in communities throughout our entire nation.

I suppose my point, sad to say, is that this is all nothing new. This week we've witnessed similar stories repeated again and again in the nightly news cycle. Yet only seldom do such instances receive the attention they deserve unless people start rioting in the streets. And when such tensions do boil over, there is no shortage of finger pointing that goes on. Republicans will blame Democrats in city government, Democrats will blame Republicans in congress, and so on and so on. The pundits and politicians mouth off at one another *ad nauseum* with shallow sound-bites and tired rhetoric, while compassionate and creative solutions to the problems facing urban America are found lacking. Using these occurrences to play politics accomplishes nothing, for the reality is that Democrats and Republicans helped make this mess together, and it's going to require the help of Democrats, Republicans and everyone else to extricate ourselves out of it.

But let's get something straight for the outset. This is not a matter of taking sides. If we feel as if we have to choose one side over another, then we have failed to make any effort to understand what's going on. In spite of what we may hear on the cable news channels or across one's twitter feed, black is not the opposite of blue. It is possible for us to support our police officers and respect the difficult work that they do while still demanding they conduct themselves ethically and responsibly. It is possible for us to sympathize with the aims of those who march our streets in protest while lamenting misguided and violent acts done out of retribution. Such matters are not mutually exclusive. There is more than enough heartbreak to go around for Alton Sterling, Philando Castile, as well as each one of those five officers in Dallas. As people of faith, we seek justice for all people. So, if we are to begin a civil and constructive dialogue surrounding racial and economic challenges in our society, then we must at least acknowledge the simple fact that this anger and frustration which is being felt in America's cities is very real—if not by us, then certainly by our neighbor.

The unjust suffering and death of any one person at the hands of the authorities might not be enough to cause social unrest in and of itself, but repeated episodes like these are merely symptoms of injustices which have been heaped upon our nation's African-American communities for generations. (And they're not alone!) For decades, we have witnessed good, well-paying manufacturing jobs being outsourced abroad, a failed drug policy, corporate tax loopholes which leave city governments holding the bag, deteriorating infrastructure, denial of opportunity in both education and the workplace, a declining middle class, and the mass proliferation of firearms. For decades, we have told lower-income families in this nation to be patient while concentrating more and more wealth in the hands of the very few with the promise that wealth might "trickle down" someday, and yet the wealth gap between rich and poor continues to grow with no change in sight. So how much longer should people be forced to wait? Another ten years? Another twenty? Fifty? Someone please tell me because people are literally *dying* for an answer!

All these elements taken together make for a volatile mix in our inner cities, and as we have seen, all it takes is a simple spark to make things explode. Stark divisions in society among races become revealed in dramatic and often tragic ways. Yet of all the gaps that exist between folks in our country, perhaps most sobering of these is the "empathy gap" found in our unwillingness to understand one another. I mean, we can spend all kinds of time identifying causes, and we can propose any number of solutions, but until we possess the courage to travel down that same road together, we will never truly comprehend the reasons for all of the anger and frustration.

When we come upon the Apostle Philip in the eighth chapter of the Book of Acts, what we bear witness to is a journey toward understanding. (Believe it or not, it is possible!) Philip is in Jerusalem when the Spirit leads him to an Ethiopian official travelling by caravan back to his homeland. The Apostle notices the eunuch struggling over the writings of the prophet Isaiah, as perhaps he did not receive the answers he was seeking while in Jerusalem. The words he recites sound eerily similar to many of the challenges that we face today, *"Like a sheep he was led to the slaughter…In his humiliation justice was denied him…For his life is taken away from the earth."*

Philip then offers his assistance by informing this Ethiopian official of the life and death of Jesus Christ, and how he too suffered and died unjustly. No one was willing to speak up for Jesus then, but now the Apostles have been tasked with spreading the Good News of Christ's resurrection to the entire world, and through baptism we have each been invited to share in this new life with our risen Lord. Intrigued, the Ethiopian eunuch sees a pool of water by the roadside and suggests perhaps he too might be baptized by the Apostle. So what does Philip do? He immediately escorts the eunuch to the water. He takes full advantage of this opportunity for reconciliation which has unexpectedly presented itself. He does not allow differences in race, differences in culture or even differences in sexuality to act as barriers to the sharing of the Holy Spirit. He does so abundantly and enthusiastically, and as result of this new understanding between strangers, the Good News begins its journey to a new land.

It has been said all good things must come to an end, and there is a certain truth to this saying. Good things do seem to have a short life span while the evils which men do have a tendency to linger. But in all honesty, good things can last a while longer with the proper care and attention. Like any delicate structure, what is good requires proper maintenance, lest our neglect allow corrosion and decay to creep in. Good relationships operate in a similar manner. They require effort, they require sacrifice, they require people to make personal investments to strengthen bonds of community. Our common humanity cannot be taken for granted. If we simply whitewash social challenges through apathy or complacency, if we simply throw up our hands and claim that there's nothing we can do, or wait until those others will admit the errors of their ways, then we remain blissfully ignorant while great chasms begin to form under our feet. Yet we should keep in mind, the next time one of these divides opens up, it could just as easily be we who find ourselves on the other side. We might actually be the ones crying out in hope of justice by declaring how our lives matter too!

Wherever these divides are found, wherever barriers exist between people, *that* is where the Holy Spirit needs to be. Are these recent tragedies going to dictate how we see one another, or are they going to serve as opportunities for reconciliation and understanding? I suppose that will be up to us. We become so accustomed to thinking of the Spirit as this "thing" "out there", we so often forget the manner in which the Holy Spirit needs to be *embodied*. It needs to have open and willing hearts to serve as vessels for righteousness. Apostles and disciples are needed who possess the courage and strength to carry the Spirit where God requires, using gifts of love and compassion to heal what has been scarred and repair what has been broken. The Spirit needs to be presented to others and shared abundantly to all who have the maturity and patience to listen. Only when we recognize one another as fellow brothers and sisters in Christ on the same journey, will we finally understand who we are in relation to one another as beloved children of God. For while people and nations sit around watching for things to slowly trickle down, the Holy Spirit commands disciples of Jesus Christ to not "wait for another day", but to "get up and go!" After all, it's a big world out there, and it's not called a "movement" for nothing.

Blessing and glory and wisdom and thanksgiving and honor and power and might be to our God forever and ever. Amen.

It was 1982 when Sharon Presbyterian called its first female associate pastor, Martha Jane Raedels, and to this day, I can still remember what a scandal it was. And yet, by the time I made it through seminary, half of the students of my graduating class were women. It just goes to show how dramatically our denomination has changed in just a few short decades. There's no question how we have been blessed by the abundant contributions of our women leaders. Many other denominations and traditions continue to lag woefully behind in this regard. Even though there is room for improvement, the willingness of the PC(USA) to be on the forefront of inclusiveness is one of the reasons I remain optimistic about our future.

Given the ever-changing nature of the church, biblical stories which portray women leaders within the early Christian movement are particularly relevant. Examples of such women are abundant in the Gospel of Luke. And although in many cases, they may remain nameless or silent, or perhaps even act as little more than foils for Jesus' teaching, their presence alone acts as a living testimony to the inclusive vision of the Good News. Perhaps this offers us some insight into the workings of the Holy Spirit, that in spite of limitations imposed upon them in their own time and throughout human history, women leaders would still find ways of making their voices heard!

Sibling Rivalry

38 Now as they went on their way, he entered a certain village, where a woman named Martha welcomed him into her home. 39She had a sister named Mary, who sat at the Lord's feet and listened to what he was saying. 40But Martha was distracted by her many tasks; so she came to him and asked, 'Lord, do you not care that my sister has left me to do all the work by myself? Tell her then to help me.' 41But the Lord answered her, 'Martha, Martha, you are worried and distracted by many things; 42there is need of only one thing. Mary has chosen the better part, which will not be taken away from her.'

Luke 10:38-42 (NRSV)

Listen up, pilgrim! Do not be fooled by this seemingly innocent little story. Appearances can be deceiving. These five lines of scripture cause more trouble than perhaps any other passage in the whole Bible. I have been engaged in many debates over many passages of scripture over my many years of ministry, but believe me, no single episode has elicited more controversy, more passion, or more raw emotion than the tale of Mary and Martha from the Gospel of Luke. Gender roles, pride, prejudices, personal relationships, sexism, sibling rivalries, faith versus works—this one has it all, my friends—fertile ground upon which to sow seeds of conflict and discontent.

The story of Mary and Martha seems harmless enough at first; Jesus and his disciples have arrived "in a certain village" where these two women have opened their home to them. We can assume that Jesus was there, being Jesus, teaching and proclaiming the Word, all while Martha's sister Mary sits at his feet listening. Naturally with a house full of out-of-town guests, these women have no shortage of responsibilities and distractions, and so Martha naturally becomes frustrated with her sister who merely sits at Jesus' feet and does nothing to help her. So, Martha comes before Jesus and accuses *him* by saying, "*Lord, do you not care…do you not care…that my sister has left me to do all the work by myself? Tell her then to help me.*" It seems a legitimate complaint, but then Jesus does not quite give her the validation she is looking for. "*Martha, Martha…You are worried and distracted by many things; there is need of only one thing. Mary has chosen the better part, which will not be taken away from her.*"

It appears from our scripture lesson that we have a quaint little tale about the importance of listening over doing. But remove this passage from the pulpit and bring it into any forum for discussion and the battle lines quickly become drawn. And strangely enough, it doesn't matter if there are two people present, or two hundred, by sheer oddity of numbers, half of the people will sympathize with Mary and the other with Martha. Mary is, after all, the listener and the learner. She is the one who stands in Christ's presence and carefully listens to her teacher. Discernment and contemplation are her priorities. Martha on the other hand, is the activist— the evangelist; she is out there working, doing the work that is necessary in service of the Lord. Both women are commendable in their respective endeavors, both are participants in Christ's ministry, so it seems odd that Jesus would validate one expression of faith over the other.

So, the question remains: Are you Mary? Or are you Martha? And this gets to the heart of why this passage becomes so controversial for so many people: When we read this passage, we become personally invested in it, as we each consider ourselves to be either listeners or doers, thinkers or activists. Those roles which we proscribe ourselves in our daily lives inform how we read scripture as well. We come to identify so much with either Mary or Martha, when Jesus finally renders his verdict upon the events of this scene, we feel personally vindicated or personally rejected as a consequence. For this reason, emotions run particularly high when discussing this passage.

In my first year of seminary I was fortunate enough to take a class about "Women in the Bible" taught by Frances Taylor-Gench. Now, in this class, women outnumbered the men twenty-four to three, and for the most part, the women were generally of one mind when considering the role gender plays in scripture. However, when the story of Mary and Martha rolled around in the syllabus one week, it was almost as if an earthquake had caused a rift right down the middle of the classroom, even among this group of women who had stood together with such solidarity. "Martha just needs to settle down and listen to Jesus like Mary," one woman would declare. To which another would reply, "But there is clearly work which needs to be done. Martha is just doing what she feels is right." To which someone else would weigh in, "Yes, but if we do things without understanding why we are doing them, aren't we simply wasting our time?" Finally, one young woman raised her hand and proclaimed, "*I blame Jesus*...Why doesn't he just get off his butt and help Martha?"

As crass as this might come across, this young woman's question raises a legitimate point (one which Martha raises herself!). After all, Jesus and his disciples are completely dependent upon the hospitality which Martha and others like her offer, so is he not being somewhat rude by taking her to task for providing that very hospitality? Is he not the direct beneficiary of her labor? But let's take matters a step further: Traditional interpretation of this story envisions Martha cooking and cleaning for her guests, coming before Jesus and Mary with an oven mitt on one hand and a rubber glove on the other, waist deep in all of the many household chores necessary for being a good hostess. But Dr. Gench was quick to remind our class how Luke makes no mention of the specific tasks in which Martha is engaged. In addition to providing for Jesus and his disciples in their journey, many early Christian congregations operated out of individual houses. Unlike today, they didn't have churches buildings with facilities or resources. It is highly probable that these two sisters were running one such, "house church" out of their home.

Think about it: That changes the story somewhat if we discover that Martha isn't distracted by mundane household chores like cooking and cleaning, but let's instead assume that she is distracted by ministering and serving, feeding the hungry, caring for the sick, assisting the poor and comforting the suffering. What does it suggest if Martha is busily engaged with those tasks which *Jesus himself* should perhaps be doing? If you look at the story that perspective, Jesus' response "Martha...silly Martha...you are distracted by many things," seems especially harsh. After all, wasn't it just a few verses earlier in the Gospel of Luke that Jesus tells the parable of the Good Samaritan? Were not his instructions to the lawyer who tested him to, *"Go and do likewise?"* [10:37] Are these not the instructions that Martha is faithfully obeying in her own ministry? Is Martha not "going and doing" as the Lord has commanded?

Perspective plays an important part in how we understand this passage, and there is great challenge in trying to see things from points-of-view which we may not have considered before. It makes one wonder how Jesus' words would be received by someone who works two jobs to provide for their children and put them through school—someone who might not have the luxury of ceasing all of their many responsibilities in favor of quiet contemplation and reflection. ("Take a 'time out'? Easy for you to say Son of Man...") Similarly, you have to wonder how this story might be perceived by a young woman discerning her own call to ministry, and when she comes across this passage in the Bible, whereas it appears Jesus' advice to men is to, "Go and do", his advice to women is essentially to, "Sit down and shut up."

And unfortunately, many Christian traditions and leaders wrongly interpret biblical stories in such a manner, treating women as little more than servants and subjects. Yet one must recognize from Luke's gospel how Mary sits at Jesus' feet in the same manner as any disciple of Jesus would have. It is hardly as if Jesus has sent her out of the room, or excused her in favor of others; rather, it is abundantly clear from this story how the women of this household have been invited—dare I even say *encouraged*—to remain in Christ's presence. Mary assumes her *rightful* place as a disciple of the Lord, and because she does this, she receives commendation. Hers is a radical act of Christian faith. She is an activist in her own right. And even in spite of Martha's many distractions, she also has been invited by the Lord to make her claim to this better part!

Maintaining proper perspective is a constant challenge for Christ's disciples, in ways both big and small. Although Martha may indeed be providing for the welfare of others, her language betrays our human inclination to become distracted. As the frustrated Martha comes before Jesus, in the course of two short sentences, she says either "me" or "myself" *four* times! Having been a pastor for some time now, I have had more than my fair share of experience with volunteer organizations, and whereas volunteering is great, volunteers themselves can be insufferable! I can tell you how easily it is for people who serve to become entrenched in their roles to the extent it becomes extraordinarily difficult, if not impossible, to welcome others in to participate. I've routinely seen new ideas and creative approaches shot down because, "That's not the way we do things." Sometimes, helping others can become all about "me" and what "I'm" doing "myself" to be a good Christian! Sometimes, we have to be reminded how our focus needs to be, not on ourselves, but on Christ, particularly the ways Christ is present among the poor, the suffering and the oppressed. Christian mission means possessing the humility to know that we still have much to learn. Even though we frequently become distracted by the many tasks and responsibilities of discipleship, men and women alike must subordinate all other priorities to the Word. The Word of the Lord is paramount, for we cannot understand our identity as Christians apart from it. Without the living Word of love and grace as our center, we risk doing things for the wrong reasons, serving our own needs, rather than our Lord's. Taking the time to listen and learn may not always prove convenient, but it is necessary, not only so we can know what tasks to do, but also in whose name we are doing them.

So now you may be thinking to yourself, "Man, now I'm really confused... So how are we supposed to act? Are we supposed to "listen and learn" as Jesus instructs Martha, or are we supposed to "go and do" as Jesus instructs the lawyer with the parable of the Good Samaritan? Obviously listening and learning is important, but we cannot always sit around and live lives of quiet contemplation, lest we also become distracted and slide into complacency (which clearly is *NOT* the better part). At some point, we've got to get out there and do some good. Even Jesus understood how he had to come down from the mountaintop, eventually. There are people out there who are hungry, there are people out there who are poor, there are people out there who are suffering or are in desperate need of justice. Are we not charged as Christ's followers to put that Word into action? When do we stop being Mary and start being Martha? Doesn't Jesus essentially contradict himself in these consecutive stories?

And yes, it is true; with the parable of the Good Samaritan followed immediately by the story of Mary and Martha, the Jesus of Luke's gospel does in fact contradict himself—but it is not without purpose. Mary and Martha are sisters after all. Just as there is a shared kinship between the two of them, there is also a shared kinship between "listening and learning" and "going and doing". And as with any sibling rivalry, there will be times when these sisters compete for our attention. There will be a time when we must "listen and learn", just as there will be a time to "go and do"; Jesus seeks to cultivate within his followers is wisdom to know when each might be appropriate!

As Christ's followers, it will be incumbent upon us to recognize when we must take time to consider matters of faith by listening carefully for the voice of our Lord. Other times, we must understand when the time for reflection has passed, and that it is once again time for Christian action—time to roll up our sleeves to "go and do" the unpleasant and often unrewarding task of the gospel. As I am often fond of saying, the Christian experience is not a quest for answers, but a search for better questions, and the contradiction between these passages raises more than their fair share. But perhaps the most important question of all might be, "What time is it now?"

Blessing and glory and wisdom and thanksgiving and honor and power and might be to our God forever and ever. Amen.

Explaining the wrath of God is complicated business. God's judgment upon nations and individuals makes us uncomfortable, so we have a tendency to favor passages which speak exclusively of God's grace and love. The Revised Common Lectionary is perhaps the greatest culprit, editing out or redacting many of the Bible's more troublesome pronouncements. Yet we cannot gloss over the fact that, as God's people, we possess a divine mandate to act in justice and righteousness, and there are significant consequences when we refuse to do so. On those occasions when God's wrath makes itself known in scripture, we must note how it never stems from random hostility or lack of concern, but out of the genuine heartbreak which is a natural extension of God's deep love. As such, we discover that judgment and grace are not opposites of one another, if anything, they are different manifestations of the same phenomenon, and we cannot pretend to lay claim to one without the other.

As the One in whom the fullness of God was pleased to dwell, Jesus Christ expressed the complexity of the divine character. Although he was also prone to moments of wrath and judgment (even toward those closest to him), Jesus' life, death and resurrection disclose how the story of the gospel is ultimately one of redemption and hope.

Dividing Lines

[Jesus said] "From everyone to whom much has been given, much will be required; and from one to whom much has been entrusted, even more will be demanded."

49 "I came to bring fire to the earth, and how I wish it were already kindled! ⁵⁰I have a baptism with which to be baptized, and what stress I am under until it is completed! ⁵¹Do you think that I have come to bring peace to the earth? No, I tell you, but rather division! ⁵²From now on, five in one household will be divided, three against two and two against three;⁵³they will be divided:

> *father against son*
> *and son against father,*
> *mother against daughter*
> *and daughter against mother,*
> *mother-in law against*
> *her daughter-in-law*
> *and daughter-in-law*

> *against mother-in-law.'*
>
> *54 He also said to the crowds, "When you see a cloud rising in the west, you immediately say, "It is going to rain"; and so it happens. 55And when you see the south wind blowing, you say, "There will be scorching heat"; and it happens. 56You hypocrites! You know how to interpret the appearance of earth and sky, but why do you not know how to interpret the present time?*
>
> Luke 12:48b-56 (NRSV)

How well do *you* know Jesus? And I only ask this, because I, for one, am not convinced that most people know Jesus the way they should. For example, I still hear this common misconception all the time, "You know, the God of the Old Testament was all about wrath and anger, but the God of the New Testament (that is, Jesus), was all about grace and love." And I suppose I can understand why people might say this. There are plenty of examples of God's wrath in the Old Testament, just as there are plenty of examples of grace and love in the New. However, we must bear in mind that we are not dealing with two separate covenants issued by two separate gods here, but a singular covenant expressed throughout time and space.

Bear with me, but my favorite (and only slightly heretical) example I frequently employ is that, no matter how you may cut it, there is only one Elvis. I know that there are people out there who say that they prefer the young, skinny "Jailhouse Rock" Elvis over the older, heavier-set "Live from Memphis, Tennessee" Elvis. But no matter how you try to parse him out, he's still the same Elvis! "Blue Moon of Kentucky" is a great song. "That's All Right" is a great song (there's no doubt about it). But "Promised Land" and "Suspicious Minds" are also great songs! There are not two Elvises (or "Elvii"), there is only one Elvis, and you cannot have one without the other. One must respect the fact, that whatever the era of his musical career, the man was a quintessential performer!

So again, let's be honest here, when we speak of grace versus wrath, or love versus judgment, we're not talking about two different gods here, but one God (in three persons) working throughout the entirety of human history. Yes, there's no denying that there is wrath in the Old Testament, but there are also numerous examples of grace and love—think of manna from heaven, water from the rock or the parting of the Red Sea. The flood cannot be understood apart from Noah and the Ark. Exile cannot be understood apart from restoration. In a similar manner, Jesus personifies grace and love, but at the same time, there are numerous examples of a Jesus who is not above showing wrath and judgment.

Take our passage for today where Jesus declares to the assembled crowds, *"I came to bring fire to the earth, and how I wish it were already kindled! Do you think that I have come to bring peace to the earth? No, I tell you, but rather division! …they will be divided: father against son / and son against father, / mother against daughter / and daughter against mother, / mother-in-law against her daughter in-law / and daughter-in-law against mother-in-law."* (Just as an interesting side note, my parents are visiting this weekend…Hi Mom and Dad!)

All kidding aside, my point to all this is that, if we are going to take seriously the benefits of divine grace and love, then we had better take seriously the reality of divine judgment and wrath, because like the God who brings them, these are not separate things. God's wrath and judgment are extensions of God's grace and mercy and we cannot possess one without the other! Accepting God's love and trusting in God's mercy means accepting God's wrath and trusting God's judgment! And I know that kind of trust is not easy to do, but, *"From everyone to whom much has been given, much will be required; and from one to whom much has been entrusted, even more will be demanded."*

Nevertheless, people want a Jesus who will satisfy our individual cravings. We want the "blessed assurance" which will let us know how wonderful and special we are. I may have mentioned this before, but I challenge any of you to venture into any bookstore in America to find the so-called "Christian" titles, and I promise you, you will have a difficult time distinguishing from the self-help section. You will find many books telling you how you can "live your best life now", how God wants you to be happy, how the Lord wants you to be fulfilled, or how through *Jee-zus*, you can find the inner peace and happiness which has managed to elude you through no fault of your own. That's the Jesus people want, a mass-marketed, focused grouped, anesthetized, domesticized Savior who will validate us and everything we already believe.

Think about it, how many times have we seen paintings or images of Jesus in story books or museums which show a "safe" Christ who is passive and docile, his compassionate visage illuminated by holy light as he prays on the mountaintop or from the Gardens of Gethsemane? How many times have we seen the bright, lily-white smile of the compassionate Christ, you know, the guy with the flowing locks of brown hair, who allows laughing children to enter into his presence or perhaps gleefully hoists a sheep upon his shoulders. We picture this patient, obedient Christ who silently bows down in humble adoration, even from the cross—a Christ who does not feel pain, a Christ oblivious to suffering or loss, a Christ who does not require anything from us. Thus, we bow our heads to pay homage to that Lackadaisical Lamb of God— the PG-13 Prince of Peace!

Yet in Luke's gospel, we receive a very different portrait of Jesus who is hot-tempered and passionate, red in the face with anger and frustration— a Jesus wholly unafraid to express his indignation, not toward heretics, doubters or unbelievers, but toward the *faithful*— beneficiaries of God's grace who should already know better! And guess what? No one's laughing now. No one is running to embrace this Jesus! This is Jesus the Revolutionary, the Usurper, the One who has come to overturn tables of oppression and balance scales of justice. And quite honestly, we don't know what to make of this person; this is not a side of Jesus that we accustomed to seeing. This is not a Jesus we are comfortable with and so we wonder why our loving and gracious Savior would suddenly lash out in such an unpredictable manner. Yet if we can't fathom why, then we must accept the possibility that our lack of understanding may be part of the problem.

Jesus did not come to congratulate us for being good and moral people. Jesus did not come to tell us just how wonderful and special we are. Jesus did not come to tell us how everything should remain the same. Does God love us? Yes. Does God care for us? Yes. Does God want the very best for us? Absolutely! But at the same time, it fair to say God wants the same for all of God's children, and the reality is, we exist in a world of great disparity (in terms of freedom, in terms of dignity and in terms of economics), where some have far more than they need while others are forced to go without. Jesus came to hold the people of God to a higher standard. God's kingdom can only come about through radical transformation and change, within both human hearts and entire societies. The *status quo* is unacceptable as long as people in our world languish under the yoke of poverty, oppression and hunger, or are given up to exploitation, addiction or despair. Those are the people for whom Christ came to offer words of consolation and hope, and it is the judgment of the Lord which calls us to act on their behalf.

Peace is the goal, it is not the means. One can imagine in the American South just a few short decades ago, a young boy asking his father, "Daddy, why do all of the black children have to go to a different school? Why do they have to sit upstairs in the movie theatre? Why do they have their own bathrooms or water fountains?" To which the father would reply, "Well son, *that's just the way things are.*" Those six words have served as our excuse for so many atrocities. Some of the worst tragedies in human history have been justified by good people passively surrendering to injustice with cold and distant hearts saying, "Well, there's nothing I can do…that's just the way things are." No doubt a similar conversation took place in Germany in the 1930's and in Rwanda in the 1990's and I wonder…I wonder…just where in our world might this conversation be taking place right now?

Jesus informs us that the way things are, are not good enough. If we are going to follow as Christ's disciples—if we are not only going to talk the talk of discipleship, but walk the walk—if we are going to *live* God's kingdom, then things have to change…*We* have to change. This cannot be accomplished by segregating ourselves apart from the rest of humanity; this cannot occur by merely sitting down and holding hands around a campfire singing "Kum-ba-yah" until our hearts' content. There is hard and difficult work to be done; there are sacrifices which *must* be made, and Jesus' words are a reminder that Christian faith is not all sunshine and daisies. Storm clouds are gathering on the horizon. Everything about us—everything about our lives and our work and our priorities—even our most fundamental human relationships must become reoriented in the service of the Lord.

With words of fervor and zeal, Jesus hopes to ignite within his followers a passion for the Good News, and stoke the flames of our hearts with discontent. As Jesus showed in his own life, true obedience to our God will bring us into direct conflict with a self-centered, idolatrous and indulgent world which happens to like things perfectly fine just the way things are. Any challenge to its authority will not be taken lightly. When you have the courage to affirm the dignity of all people, when you acknowledge our common humanity, when you demand justice, fairness and compassion for the very least of these, then (also as Jesus showed) the world will push back and push back hard! Yet as these conflicts become inevitable, by placing ourselves in direct tension with the world that is, we express confidence in the world that is to come—that God's judgment is true and victory assured. When all is said and done, grace and love reign supreme, for what God has ordained since the beginning, so it shall be in the end.

So again I ask, how well do we know Jesus? How prepared are we to receive the Word (and by that, I mean the *true* Word…not some watered down, anemic version of the Gospel, but that red-blooded, burning Gospel that calls all people to repentance)? How ready are we for the Christ who has the audacity to call even our most fundamental beliefs and relationships into question? There were plenty of people in Jesus' day who would tell him, "Oh no, you shouldn't say that…People don't want to listen to that. Hey Jesus, if you know what's good for you, you'll keep your opinions to yourself!"

Little do such people realize, the Gospel is meant to offend. When God's people have become complacent or self-absorbed, the Gospel is meant to highlight our collective shortcomings and illustrate our personal need for divine grace. Jesus came to set the world on fire, but these are not just fires of wrath and judgment, but also fires of life and Spirit. This is the fire which has been entrusted to us, so that it might set our hearts ablaze with renewed zeal for love and service in God's name. The same fire burns away barriers which separate people from one another, that we may recognize how we are one family, brothers and sisters in Jesus Christ. And you can run, but you can't hide. There is no shelter, nor is there any refuge from the coming fire, as everyone has been called to love and act as God's people. The judgment of the Lord is the promise that there is such a thing as justice, there is such a thing as accountability, but if we can find it within ourselves to trust God with these difficult and ominous things, how much easier will it be for us to place trust in God's mercy and forgiveness as well?

At my former church, the youth and would always tell one another: "Don't start nothin', there won't be nothin'." And most often this expression would serve as cautionary reminder to keep us out of trouble. But in spite of my blatant use of a double-negative (or quadruple-negative, as the case may be), the adage is true; if you don't start anything, there won't ever be anything. Sometimes we as Christians are called to be peacemakers, but at other times, we are called to get into a little trouble for the sake of the Gospel—to stand up and be counted for what is right, regardless of cost. Doing the right thing is not always popular, and in some instances, it may even cause conflict with those dearest to us. But conflict is never the end of the world. Sometimes conflict can be an avenue for creative possibility, providing new opportunities for knowledge and mutual understanding. As faith calls our most sacred relationships into question, so too can faith show us the reality of reconciliation and restoration.

So (in the spirit of the Olympic Games) as you go about your lives this week, remember that fire that has been passed along to you. Remember the gift with which you have been entrusted— and should the opportunity present itself, then who knows? Maybe you can even light a little fire of your own. Bear in mind this little twist upon the wisdom of our youth, "Start something, and there *will be* something."

Blessing and glory and wisdom and thanksgiving and honor and power and might be to our God forever and ever. Amen.

The Christian faith is not a quest for answers. If that is all we seek, then we will inevitably be found wanting. I have always taught that the Christian faith is about our willingness to ask better questions. Perhaps it's no accident that biblical passages over which I struggle with most, seem to produce some of my best work. Great sermons are honest sermons which do not run away from the more troublesome aspects of Christian faith. Therefore, I greatly appreciate those passages which are able to knock me from my comfort zone, and force me toward a deeper understanding of text and message.

In particular, I've always been uncomfortable with the idea that God "tests" people—that God places physical or spiritual obstacles in our way as a means of evaluating our character. Theological problems abound with such a quandary, and unfortunately, many Christians are still wed to a Pharisaic mindset which tells them that the good health or good fortune they enjoy are the direct result of individual piety. At least on the surface, the God of scripture who constantly "tests" people would appear to lend credence to this. Yet we must possess the courage to look deeper, while also avoiding the other theological extreme, where a disinterested God simply abandons God's people to fate. Stories of Job, Abraham and Isaac, and Joseph and his brothers force us to consider many uncomfortable questions surrounding God's providence versus human agency, to which belong no easy answers. But I suppose some comfort may be found, not in the tests themselves, but in the purposes for which they are given. God doesn't test us to show our righteousness, God does it to show God's!

This is yet another sermon delivered to the good folks at our local retirement community, many of whom face significant physical and mental challenges which come naturally from aging. Even throughout times of helplessness and uncertainty, we place faith in a God who is constantly at work on our behalf, providing us with what we need to persevere.

The Unkindest Cut

1 After these things God tested Abraham. He said to him, 'Abraham!' And he said, 'Here I am.' ²He said, 'Take your son, your only son Isaac, whom you love, and go to the land of Moriah, and offer him there as a burnt-offering on one of the mountains that I shall show you.' ³So Abraham rose early in the morning, saddled his donkey, and took two of his young men with him, and his son Isaac; he cut the wood for the burnt-offering, and set out and went to the place in the distance that God had shown him. ⁴On the third day Abraham looked up and saw the place far away. ⁵Then Abraham said to his young men, 'Stay here with the donkey; the boy and I will go over there; we will worship, and then we will come back to you.' ⁶Abraham took the wood of the burnt-offering and laid it on his son Isaac, and he himself carried the fire and the knife. So the two of them walked on together. ⁷Isaac said to his father Abraham, 'Father!' And he said, 'Here I am, my son.' He said, 'The fire and the wood are here, but where is the lamb for a burnt offering?' ⁸Abraham said, 'God himself will provide the lamb for a burnt-offering, my son.' So, the two of them walked on together. 9 When they came to the place that God had shown him, Abraham built an altar there and laid the wood in order. He bound his son Isaac, and laid him on the altar, on top of the wood. ¹⁰Then Abraham reached out his hand and took the knife to kill his son. ¹¹But the angel of the Lord called to him from heaven, and said, 'Abraham, Abraham!' And he said, 'Here I am.' ¹²He said, 'Do not lay your hand on the boy or do anything to him; for now, I know that you fear God, since you have not withheld your son, your only son, from me.' ¹³And Abraham looked up and saw a ram, caught in a thicket by its horns. Abraham went and took the ram and offered it up as a burnt-offering instead of his son. ¹⁴So Abraham called that place 'The Lord will provide'; as it is said to this day, 'On the mount of the Lord it shall be provided.'

Genesis 22:1-14 (NRSV)

I don't deal well with frustration. Truth be told, I never really lose my temper unless I find myself in a situation where there is no easy way out, or that I've managed to do something stupid and have no one else to blame but myself. You see, I consider myself somewhat of a proactive personality. When presented with a problem, somewhere in my brain I believe that I can turn any situation to my advantage that it is a simple matter of taking appropriate measures.

But as I have to be reminded of from time to time, life is seldom so kind or predictable. Sometimes you find yourself in a situation where there simply is no way out, and there is no amount of creativity that will extricate yourself from that situation. Even for a dyed-in-the-wool Calvinist, it is hard for me to accept that there are some things beyond my control.

Case in point…When I was younger, I had a huge crush on this beautiful girl. We would spend time with each other, and we would always have a great time talking and laughing, and we always looked forward to when we would see one another again. But her life was complicated, in that she had just broken up with someone, and she was starting at a new school, and that she wasn't prepared to get emotionally invested in another relationship so soon.

We weren't exactly dating, but for all intents and purposes, I felt as if she had broken up with me, and that there was nothing I could do to make things any different. I couldn't change her situation any more than I could roll back time. I was frustrated, and angry, heartbroken, and this caused a once cherished friendship to sour into resentment.

I eventually got even with her, though…I married her.

All kidding aside, I don't know about you, but I find the story of Abraham's sacrifice of Isaac to be extremely frustrating. There appears to be no place one can turn to find solace in a story that seems so cruel. "Seems" …Ha! This story doesn't seem cruel, it **is** cruel, this whole idea that Abraham must sacrifice his son, with no explanation and no justification for such a horrible act.

As a pastor, I understand how God calls us to obey God's will, and to place all things in service to our Lord. I understand that God demands sacrifice, if we are willing to, not just profess faith, but to live that faith in the world. I understand…I get that. But I don't feel as though I could sacrifice my loved ones any more than I could sacrifice this selfsame love of God, for it is through those dearest to me that the love of God is best and most deeply experienced. To sever those bonds either figuratively or literally for absolutely no reason whatsoever—there seems no greater sacrilege. I for one, am unable to separate the love of God from the love of others, and to bear witness to this story as Abraham pulls back the knife to obey God's command, even though no blood is ever drawn, truly this is the unkindest cut of all!

And when folks hear this story, we typically dismiss or rationalize the violence, believing that God never really intends for Abraham to sacrifice his son. Like heroes of old, we trust that God will swoop in at the last second to save Isaac from this terrible fate. And why? Because the sacrifice of a child goes against everything we believe about God, so our minds have to grasp for a satisfactory answer. "Oh, God would never to that…God's just *testing* Abraham!" But try offering that consolation to a scared boy who has the cold steel of his father's blade pressed firmly against his throat. "C'mon Isaac! Where's your sense of humor? Don't you *get it?*" If this is what God intends, then the whole episode seems little more than a cruel and heartless joke.

You see what I mean? Frustration. No way out. Either God is serious about sacrificing Isaac, which would make God cruel and heartless, or God is just kidding around, which would make God…well, cruel and heartless. But I don't believe God to be cruel, I don't believe God to be heartless, and I certainly don't believe that God has some sick sense of humor, or is petty enough to be satisfied by tokens of human blood.

What I find most distasteful about this passage is this idea that God tests people—that God might use human suffering as some moral barometer. And I tell this all the time to people who face real struggles in life. I don't believe that God tests people by giving them cancer or heart disease, I don't believe that God gauges faith through the suffering of children. I don't believe that God throws depression or addiction, mental illness or physical disability in our way just as a means of building our character. I don't believe this. *I will* **never** *believe this!* And yet at the end of the day, when all is said and done, much to my frustration, there it is staring at me in cold, black, Times New Roman font, "God *tested* Abraham."

So, you know what? You may never hear me say this again, but I give up. If God is unwilling to offer a reasonable explanation for God's demands, then I don't see why I should have to! So, if any of you were expecting this pastor to provide a nice, clean, safe explanation for why Abraham had to sacrifice his son to appease the Lord—if you need a rationale to discover why the covenant of the Lord would hang so precariously in the balance, then I'm afraid I've got nothing for you. Because that's the problem: This is not a nice, clean or safe passage. This is one fraught with questions, mystery and doubt. There is no safe little message in here that one can wrap up in a neat little package and tie a bow around it. In the end, this story is disturbing, unsettling and frustrating, just as it was meant to be.

And I'm afraid that's the best I can do, is to focus upon how this passage is intended. As with many stories in the bible, the purpose may not be to offer us a clear and satisfying answer, as much as it is to offer us some insight into the mystery of our Lord which lies just beyond the veil—that odd combination of human will and divine intervention that eludes our capacity to fully understand it. Perhaps this passage intends to teach us something; not about ourselves— not about our capacity to obey the will of God—not our willingness to blindly follow the commands of some mysterious deity. This passage teaches us nothing about our strengths, our character, or our morality. Too often we read these troubling passages and assume they're trying to teach us something about ourselves, but this is seldom the case at all. As we have to be reminded, it's not about us. This passage (like all others) intends to teach us something about God.

And I think—I *believe*—the message of this passage is that the Lord will provide. It's not neat and it's not pretty, but the Lord will provide. In times of weakness, throughout times of doubt, even during times of trouble or irrational, unexplainable chaos, God will provide us with what we need to persevere. Now, it may not arrive in some nice, neat easy-to-explain package to our satisfaction, yet in the end, the Lord will provide, for obedience to God is never easy. It will force us into difficult decisions and may even bring us into conflict with those closest to us. And for all of the challenges that arise as a consequence of living a life of true faith—for all of the love and relationships that we must be willing to sacrifice to live in obedience to God's commands—the Lord provides us with the means to restore those relationships and to make us whole once again, strengthening us and the ones we love so the people of God may together continue our journey toward the fulfillment of God's promises.

God tested Abraham. Try as we might, we cannot escape this. But in the end, it wasn't Abraham who passed the test. He didn't have to. Abraham was **relieved** of this obligation, just as we all have been. God passed the test for us by providing the most worthy sacrifice of all. It wasn't Isaac's death, but the death of God's own Son that would forever reveal the true measure of righteousness. Christ's death put an end to the testing and the sacrifices once and for all; Christ is the One through whom the wrath of God is satisfied, not through numerous acts of violence and divine retribution, but by one singular act of love. It is through Christ that reconciliation is possible, and that we as a family once again are made complete. Perhaps there is great comfort in that we place faith in a God who doesn't just ask for sacrifice, but is willing to sacrifice so much for us. This might actually be the most frustrating part of all, that we would owe so much to someone else for this gift of our redemption.

Blessing and glory and wisdom and thanksgiving and honor and power and might be to our God forever and ever. Amen.

This is a sermon about our human tendency to live the moment—quite appropriate for a sermon on the Letter to the Hebrews. After all, Hebrews is so theologically and Christologically unique that it can only be fully understood within a certain historical and cultural light. A product of its own time and place, it was written in a period of great transformation for the church, as the rapid expansion of the Christian faith began to sputter under increased social and religious scrutiny. Although this was a period of great anxiety, it provided occasion for the church to adapt to present circumstance by reevaluating what it meant to be God's reconciling community of faith.

As the church moves further into the 21st century, it's striking to note the similarities between the post-Christendom church and challenges faced during the Apostolic age. We too are presently experiencing a period when people are falling away from Christianity in great numbers, and like then, our ability to persevere in faith assumes a greater urgency. Hebrews is well-suited as a reference in this regard, encouraging the faithful to broaden our vision to see God's redemptive activity as it occurs throughout human history and into the present age, on the way to something greater.

As I am always telling my congregation, we have to be the church we are, not the church we were twenty or thirty years ago. Nor can Christian mission be centered around what we assume our church will look like in the decades to come. We should definitely honor our past and plan for the future, but first and foremost, discipleship dictates that we do our part to be responsive to the needs of our time and place.

Forget Me Not

13 Let mutual love continue. ^{2}Do not neglect to show hospitality to strangers, for by doing that some have entertained angels without knowing it. ^{3}Remember those who are in prison, as though you were in prison with them; those who are being tortured, as though you yourselves were being tortured. ^{4}Let marriage be held in honor by all, and let the marriage bed be kept undefiled; for God will judge fornicators and adulterers. ^{5}Keep your lives free from the love of money, and be content with what you have; for he has said, 'I will never leave you or forsake you.' ^{6}So we can say with confidence, 'The Lord is my helper; I will not be afraid.

What can anyone do to me?'

> *7 Remember your leaders, those who spoke the word of God to you; consider the outcome of their way of life, and imitate their faith. 8Jesus Christ is the same yesterday and today and forever. 15Through him, then, let us continually offer a sacrifice of praise to God, that is, the fruit of lips that confess his name. 16Do not neglect to do good and to share what you have, for such sacrifices are pleasing to God.*
>
> Hebrews 13:1-8, 15-16 (NRSV)

Human nature displays an uncanny knack for living in the moment. And I suppose this can be a good thing, for the most part. There is something to be said for freshness and spontaneity, celebrating life the present, unbound by habit or custom. Originality and creativity certainly have their treasured place in our life together as the Body of Christ. As a pastor, I always make it a point to try to encourage this congregation to be the church in the present and not the church of the past, to consider who God is calling us to be for our time and place. And whereas living in the moment can be a wonderful and inspirational gift, like so many things about our human nature, it is something which must be maintained with proper balance. Live too much in the present, and we risk forgetting the past or neglecting the future. The same part of us which compels us to want to live for today, can sometimes… sometimes…provide us with very short memories.

I suppose the best way I can describe this, is that when we are blessed with good health, sometimes we can forget what it is like to be sick. When we enter into good fortune, sometimes we may forget what it was like to once go without. When we enjoy the many blessings of family or friendship, how quickly memories of loneliness or heartache fade from recollection. Of course, the corollary to this formula is that, when we find ourselves alone, we quickly forget what it means to enjoy fellowship or friendship. When we are struggle financially, we sometimes forget what it is like to prosper. When we are sick or suffering, it can be difficult to remember what it is like to be healthy and strong. When we give into cynicism and despair, we forget what it is like to live in anticipation and hope. Present circumstance has an annoying habit of dictating how we perceive ourselves relative to the world around us.

The letter to the Hebrews was written during a time of great uncertainty in the life of the Christian faith. Many decades had passed since Christ's early days in Galilee. The first generation of Apostles was starting to pass away, and the growth of this now global church began to meet increased resistance from both within and without. Granted, this was long before the great systematic persecutions of the 3rd century in the Roman Empire, but nevertheless, Christians living during this era were starting to experience (at least on a local level) increased social scrutiny and ostracism, subject to the prejudices of what was considered "acceptable" society at large. Antipathy and even violence toward Christ's followers would become more and more commonplace as the years went on. If a natural disaster occurred somewhere through drought or disease, local pagan priests or politicians would rally support by making Christians the scapegoat, accusing them of violating their traditional Roman values. Moreover, to make matters even more complicated, as each day passed, promises of Jesus' inevitable return in the flesh would appear to go unfulfilled, causing many Christians to doubt the long-term prospects of this emerging faith.

Under the weight of increasing social and political pressures, many new converts began abandoning the Christian faith in droves. "What has Christ ever done for me?" they would lament. "Why should I have to bear scorn and scars from others while receiving nothing in return?" The letter to the Hebrews was written in the hopes of stemming the tide of this exodus, encouraging members of this new covenant to hold fast and persevere by reminding them of the reasons why they became part of this faith to begin with. When times were good and Christians essentially, "flew under the radar" of society at large, there wasn't much of a problem. They could enjoy the benefits of Christian fellowship and grace free from the scrutiny of the powers-that-be. However, as time passed and as principles of faith and life in true community brought them into conflict with a society centered on the self, that's when many began to rethink their association to this person called the Christ—the memory of promises of justice, rebirth and renewal having quickly faded just as soon as the going got tough.

How easily we forget! How quickly principle becomes abandoned in the face of the slightest amount of scrutiny! Two thousand years may have passed, and much has indeed changed, but human nature pretty much remains the same. People today are certainly abandoning the Christian faith in droves, ushering in a new era of uncertainty. For centuries Protestantism preached freedom of conscience, so what do we do when conscience leads people away from the church? Therefore, this same advice to the early Christian community to hold fast in faith echoes throughout the ages for those living today. "Remember," Hebrews reminds this fickle and flawed people,

"Remember who you are and to whom you belong." Remember God's steadfast love, and all that God has done and is doing for God's people. Remember how necessary it is to strive for the good, to labor in the cause of justice, and honor promises of faithfulness we have made to one another. Anyone can trust in God when times are good, but when times are tough, that is when God needs genuine people of good faith willing to stand up and be counted for what is right!

When times are tough, how often we forget when times are good. And when times are good, how quickly we forget how times can be challenging. Should we live exclusively in the moment, we risk slipping into short-sightedness, unable to see how our actions, or lack thereof, effect those around us. Hebrews encourages the people of God to broaden our vision, for as bad as we think we may have it, it stands to reason that there are those in the world who have it infinitely worse than we do.

How blessed and how comfortable we must be, when even the slightest possibility of discomfort becomes too much for us to bear! Americans are frequently informed how Christianity is being "persecuted" in this country, and yet there are documented instances of people around the world who know first-hand what true persecution means, as they live each day in places where openly professing faith in Christ is tantamount to a death sentence. When we yammer on and on about how personal liberties and freedoms are being threatened, how conveniently we forget that there are real people languishing in prisons in our nation who have been unjustly convicted, denied due process of law, or given cruel and unusual sentences for victimless crimes. (Fortunately for us, we don't place faith in a god who adheres to a strict "three strikes and you're out" policy.) Hebrews hopes that, even in the midst our own suffering, we might bear such people in our hearts and minds as well, because we are all in this together. Throughout times of comfort and throughout times of challenge, we as Christ's body are reminded of our calling to proclaim the Good News to the world, recommitting ourselves to the often thankless and unpopular task of lending strength to the powerless and voice to the voiceless.

It seems as if we have short memories when it comes to the many blessings we enjoy, but my, oh my, how long we can carry a grudge when we feel the least bit insulted or offended! How long we wait in restless anticipation for that day when the tables will finally be turned, and that we can repay others with interest for wrongs which have been inflicted upon us. Yet Hebrews also reminds us, that as true followers of Jesus Christ, we have to let our petty need for vengeance go. We have to let go of the hatred and the anger, we have to release the pain and the bitterness, we have to learn to forgive—and not just for their sake, but for our own. We have to get right with God to acknowledge the ways in which we have fallen short, that we might free ourselves from shackles of perpetual victimhood to be empowered servants of the Almighty. Hebrews confirms how we trust in a God of justice, that everyone will ultimately answer for each offense which has been inflicted. Can we trust God enough to leave such matters in God's hands? Do we truly believe it when God tells us, "I will never leave or forsake you"? As the pain of human shortsightedness becomes increasingly apparent in the world, so too does love need to abound all the more.

This week, our nation was treated to a small serving of irony when the home of a famous evangelical pastor was flooded as a result of the recent rains in Louisiana. Prior to the flooding, this pastor had been notorious for claiming in sermons and public discourse that God sends hurricanes and floods to punish the United States for our nation's increasing tolerance of homosexuality. How strange it is when Christians fail to recollect the time in our history when that particular shoe was tied firmly to our other foot! What I hope we (as well as this aforementioned pastor) might remember from this experience, is that natural disasters are not punishments directed at people for alleged shortcomings, but rather opportunities for those who claim to be faithful servants of God to "go and do" the difficult work of the gospel—to not turn a blind eye, or offer superficial judgment, but to openly and abundantly share mutual love and gifts with people in need regardless of circumstance. Perhaps we can all use this occasion to recall words from scripture which describe a compassionate and loving God who hears the cries of all who are in distress, who delivers God's people from the rising waters, who comforts us throughout all our sorrows and restores us all to the promise of a better tomorrow.

Forgetfulness breeds ingratitude. This is precisely what Hebrews hopes to warn us against: Forgetfulness breeds ingratitude. However, when we show ourselves to be selfless, hospitable, charitable, gracious and compassionate, we express appreciation to our Lord for all that has been done for us. In sacrificing of ourselves freely and generously, we recall the example of the One who was willing to sacrifice everything that God's will for the world might be accomplished. Hebrews advice for life together is simple: Allow relationships to be true. Let love be genuine. Forsake trust in money and material things. Most of all, Hebrews simply wants us to remember—*remember*. Perhaps that's not too much to ask for, that as disciples of Jesus Christ, we remember who we are and to whom we belong. Regardless of what challenges we may face in this life, God assures us that our present circumstance will always be one of abundant forgiveness and grace, yesterday, today and forever. This knowledge alone dictates how we as both individuals and a community should engage this world and those who live in it. Humble expressions of gratitude and mutual love show a forgetful world that at least our memory is still intact!

Blessing and glory and wisdom and thanksgiving and honor and power and might be to our God forever and ever. Amen.

I consider myself blessed that I've never known true poverty. Even as a former "starving artist" and seminary graduate, I've known a few lean years, but I've never had to experience the indignity of wondering how I was going to pay the rent, or where my next meal was coming from—nothing even close. But now that I and my wife have become established within our respective vocations, it's odd how we find ourselves frequently reminiscing about simpler times. Like most couples, we didn't have a lot of money when we were first starting out, but our needs were far simpler. Most of all, we had time and the freedom to do the things we wanted to do, or go where we wanted to go. Granted, hindsight may be overromanticizing things, but it's ironic that we worked so hard to achieve a certain station in life, yet now that we have it, we aspire return to some semblance of a more carefree time. To accomplish this, we understand there are certain things we would have to give up, yet our human need for security and stability dictates otherwise. Scaling back and simplifying proves complicated enough, so what are we to do with a Christ who ups the ante by demanding that we give up everything for the sake of the Good News? It would be wise not to assume that Jesus speaks hypothetically or hyperbolically when it comes to the dangers posed by material wealth. Christians truly have a tendency to take some passages of scripture too literally, while others, we do not take literally enough! We live with the knowledge that we'll have to give up everything eventually. In the meantime, we must consider what in life is holding us back and preventing us from following in Christ's way.

Moving Day

25 Now large crowds were travelling with him; and he turned and said to them, 26 Whoever comes to me and does not hate father and mother, wife and children, brothers and sisters, yes, and even life itself, cannot be my disciple. 27Whoever does not carry the cross and follow me cannot be my disciple. 28For which of you, intending to build a tower, does not first sit down and estimate the cost, to see whether he has enough to complete it? 29Otherwise, when he has laid a foundation and is not able to finish, all who see it will begin to ridicule him, 30saying, "This fellow began to build and was not able to finish." 31Or what king, going out to wage war against another king, will not sit down first and consider whether he is able with ten thousand to oppose the one who comes against him with twenty thousand?32If he cannot, then, while the other is still far away, he sends a delegation and asks for the terms of peace. 33So therefore, none of you can become my disciple if you do not give up all your possessions.

Luke 14:25-33 (NRSV)

Several years ago, I was visiting the home of a parishioner who was transitioning to a retirement community in Richmond. It was sad to see her leave our congregation in Buena Vista, of course, but relocating to Richmond meant that she would be closer to her family, the grandchildren, and the community had the resources to provide for her needs at this stage of her life. And so I dropped by one afternoon before the big move, and the house was cluttered throughout with various sizes of cardboard boxes with the memories of an entire lifetime contained therein. Bookshelves, cedar chests and bedframes were poised to go right out the front door, this one marked for the new apartment, this one marked for storage, etc. etc. And so as we sat on a couch in a near-empty room, one of the first questions I asked her was to inquire how the move was going, and with an exasperated look on her face, she replied, "I know you're still young, but take my advice; start giving away all your possessions *now*!"

Sage advice indeed, especially for someone like myself who comes from a long line of pack rats.

If any of you have ever had the courage to venture inside my office, you know of which I speak. Indeed, that may be the most insidious thing about our possessions, in that they seem to accumulate gradually, over time...so invisibly that we hardly even notice. I think this is one more thing we can chalk it up to human nature, for we are all guilty of this in one way or another. Perhaps that's why people have a tendency to stay put, that way, we can avoid acknowledging a certain truth as to the abundance of possessions. We don't actually realize how much we've accumulated until we reach a period of transition in our lives, at which point we are often found standing around a pile of boxes scratching our heads wondering, "How in the world did I get so much *stuff*?"

Comedian George Carlin once put it this way, *"That's all you need in life, a little place for your stuff. That's all your house is—If you didn't have so much stuff, you wouldn't need a house. You could just walk around all the time...And when you leave your house, you gotta lock it up. Wouldn't want somebody to come by and take some of your stuff...That's what your house is, a place to keep your stuff while you go out and get...more stuff?"*[1]

Although he is being silly, Mr. Carlin drives home a very serious point. In many ways, the things which we own only represent the tip of the proverbial iceberg. One can only imagine the volume of resources we expend year after year, decade after decade, generation after generation, just so we can hang on to what's ours! From fences to door locks to barbed wire to security systems to firearms to insurance policies to banks and wills and trusts, there are entire industries dedicated to keeping our possessions in the proper fold! We spend trillions of our tax dollars on defense and develop ever increasingly creative ways to kill one another—we undermine foreign governments and manipulate global markets, just so those people over there won't come take our stuff over here!

But allow me to reel myself back in for just a moment: Why do we need—or should I say, why do we *feel the need* to have so many possessions? Well, I'm not really sure. That's an interesting question for philosophers and psychologists alike. Human beings, are by our nature, very insecure creatures, and I think, for most folks, possessions offer a certain measure of security which may otherwise elude us. Possessions serve as tangible reminders to ourselves and to others of our social standing in life, essentially telling others a visual story of our accomplishments. And through the things we accumulate we seek to shape that narrative, showing ourselves to the world, not necessarily as we are, but as we want to be. That's why we always want the newest and the latest and the highest quality. We desire things that are precious, rare and decidedly unique, because that's how we wish to be seen! And so, we surround ourselves with things that illustrate to the world that we are shrewd, cultured and sophisticated with, "...*an appreciation for fine craftsmanship and intricate detail*..."

So, in theory, with enough effort and resources, we should be able to find that odd collection of merchandise which reflects our tastes and our sensibilities at any given moment in our life. But therein lies the catch—human beings are not static creatures, but we are constantly changing and evolving, and at least on some subconscious level, I think we are aware of this fact. Therefore, this story we seek to communicate is constantly being forced to change as well, and it tries its best to keep up with little avail. As it so happens, every single one of us is such a complex, intricate and so wonderfully complicated a creature, that no number of things can ever possibly serve as an adequate representation of who we actually are. And eventually, we all reach that unavoidable critical mass in our lives where possessions can no longer keep up with the changes. Sometime this realization is gradual; sometimes it's traumatic. Maybe it's caused by a move, switching jobs, an empty nest, or the loss of a loved one. Only at these transitional moments in life are we offered a sobering reminder of the relative worth of "things".

Such moments can be beneficial, because they afford us the opportunity to take stock of our priorities. It's interesting to note, that of all the many hard and difficult demands that Jesus makes of his disciples (such as laying down one's life for one another, taking up the cross, forgiving one's enemy, etc.), why does it seem as if giving up our possessions is the most difficult one of all? Any one of us here can think of countless examples of people who have risked their lives for strangers, those who have suffered grievously for their faith, and those who have accomplished indescribable acts of forgiveness for the most heinous of offenses, but I would wager very few of us can think of anyone...*anyone*, who has literally given away all that they have in the name of Jesus Christ! One might think that divesting ourselves of our various possessions (as well as the many burdens which comes along with them) would actually be the *easiest* of all these. Now you have it, now you don't! No harm done. Yet, this is hardly, if ever, the case! I mean sure, we all assume we can do it if we *had* to, and some folks may have even tried on rare occasion, and still, I am reminded of Linus and his blue security blanket, who so bravely tosses away his most beloved possession just to prove something to his sister Lucy. Yet, as the minutes begin to tick away and the reality of his situation becomes apparent—as soon as that insecurity begins to seep back into the recesses of his mind—Linus starts to shake and to sweat, and out of panic and desperation, he goes sprinting full-throttle back to his blanket just as fast as his stubby little legs can carry him.

Linus' attachment to possessions serves as a metaphor for our own. And why is this? Why can't we shake this *addiction* to material goods? Why do we feel as if we cannot live without them? I believe it's largely because things like laying down our lives for one another, and taking up the cross, and loving our enemy as ourselves...we are relatively comfortable with such things because we know that they are within our control. I know that sounds strange to say, but even should we be unsure of anything else, at the very least, we can trust ourselves to at least *try* to do what Jesus asks. Giving up our many possessions, though, is considerably more difficult because this involves a different kind of trust; this involves trust in the *other*. This means relinquishing control; this means leaving ourselves vulnerable. This requires placing our trust in our neighbor that our needs will be taken care of and that we will be provided for. This means placing our trust in God that our many sacrifices would not be in vain. This means expressing our hope that the presence of the Holy Spirit is real, and through the kindness and compassion working through others, we may in some small way bear witness to the coming kingdom of our Lord.

Such faith in God and such faith in others would seem extraordinary by human standards. And yet according to Jesus, such sacrifice is not a byproduct of being saintly or pious, but it is a simple matter of common sense! Jesus poses the question: Do we not make use of such common sense in the course of our daily lives? Before undertaking some personal project or cause, do we not at least take a moment to consider the costs involved relative to the benefit received? If possessions weigh us down and prevent us from going out and serving the Lord, then, really...of what worth are they? What is the value of temporary comforts when weighed against the mere *possibility* of eternity? Jesus instructs us to do the math. True disciples possess the courage to give up everything to follow Christ—and not just in terms of our belongings, but even those very relationships of family and friendship which we believe so foundational to our identity. As important as such things may be to us, we must be willing to leave it all behind, lest the things we own end up owning us instead!

Maybe that's the point Jesus is trying to make. Perhaps the problem is not so much our possessions, but the claim which they have upon our lives. For all their power, for all of their appeal, the one thing they can never do is justify. Only faith can do that. By essentially shocking us into submission, perhaps Jesus is suggesting to his followers that we should allow the voice of our Lord to guide us forward, rather than becoming mired by the fear of what might happen to us if we suddenly lost it all. (Let's face it, if you don't have anything, then you don't have anything to lose!) I'm confident in saying we have all experienced how possessions can act as barriers to mutual love and fellowship, ensnaring us through debt and constant obligation. Churches are notoriously vulnerable to this. If all of our conversations involve how to best care for our stuff, instead of others, then we need to take a long, serious look at what exactly is holding us back. For the life of the disciple has never been one of staying put, but it means having the courage to go forth to love and serve the Lord. Traveling light, therefore, is essential to Christian mission. Jesus devoted his life and ministry going from place to place to touch people in need, and he refused to allow anything to prevent him from proclaiming the Good News to the world.

If you will notice in the Gospel of Luke, Jesus and his disciples are in perpetual motion. They are constantly travelling from one place to the next, and sometimes it can even seem as if they are roaming around in circles. To the untrained eye, they appear to wander aimlessly, yet Jesus is still leading his followers somewhere, even as they often fail to understand the reasons behind it all. As outlandish as his demands can be, the disciples still have to place their trust him to get to their destination. And as part of this journey, Jesus Christ informs us that there is a direct relationship between the things we own and our capacity to follow. In no uncertain terms, he declares, *"None of you can become my disciple if you do not give up* **all** *(not part…not most…but ALL) your possessions."* (His words, not mine!) Discipleship is not about what we get to keep, but what we are willing to give up for the sake of the gospel. Christ showed how he was willing to give up everything for us, and if we truly want to walk that same road, then we have to do what we can to try to keep up.

Now, as I mentioned a few weeks ago, it may be too much to ask us to be exactly like Jesus; but that shouldn't suggest for one moment that we cannot be a little *more* like Jesus. We can begin by making a sincere effort to live more simply, without relying upon the false security offered by material wealth or large amounts of stuff. We can consume a little less, and perhaps give back a little more. We can be a little less stubborn and intransigent, to discover new ways of depending upon one another instead. Perhaps by keeping our burdens light, we can be ready at a moment's notice to venture where our Lord calls.

Blessing and glory and wisdom and thanksgiving and honor and power and might be to our God forever and ever. Amen.

1. George Carlin, "A Place for My Stuff", *A Place for My Stuff*, Atlantic Records, 1981.

Being married to an attorney, the subject of justice comes up a lot in our conversations. As different as our respective work environments may be, the pursuit of justice is the one thing our vocations share in common. It's interesting how both disciplines strive mightily toward some divinely inspired ideal, and yet human nature routinely reveals them to be imperfect and flawed in their application.

Nevertheless, in both the legal and ecclesiastical realms, we are reminded of the importance of language—that it's not just what you say, but the way that you say it. In spite of its obvious limitations, language has power—far more power than I think most people realize. It can inspire the mind and stir the soul, but it can also exploit and marginalize. Therefore, I have little patience for those who use language haphazardly or abusively. Words and stories help shape our identity and unite us within a common history and culture. If we are to create a nation and a church where all people have equal access to justice, the we must be cognizant of not only how language is offered, but how it may be received. This is not a matter of "political correctness", but basic human decency. Unfortunately, there are those in the public sphere who cower behind the First Amendment to our Constitution, justifying cruel and oppressive language under a guise of "honesty". In doing so, they take the absolute worst aspect of our human character and attempt to pass it off as virtue.

God is not fooled. Perversion of the divine gift of language will require accountability. "You shall go to all to whom I send you, / and you shall speak whatever I command you," says the Lord to the prophet [Jer. 1:7]. God empowers prophets with language because of language's power to effect transformative change, and God commands us to speak words of hope and consolation to society's most vulnerable. The Word of the Lord not only promises justice for the oppressed, but also for the oppressor as well—assuming, of course, we have the wisdom and courage to listen!

Just Desserts

18 My joy is gone, grief is upon me, my heart is sick.

19 Hark, the cry of my poor people from far and wide in the land: 'Is the Lord not in Zion?

  Is her King not in her?'

('Why have they provoked me to anger with their images, with their foreign idols?')

20 'The harvest is past, the summer is ended, and we are not saved.'

> 21 For the hurt of my poor people I am hurt, I mourn, and dismay has taken hold of me.
> 22 Is there no balm in Gilead?
> Is there no physician there?
> Why then has the health of my poor people not been restored?
>
> 9:1 O that my head were a spring of water, and my eyes a fountain of tears, so that I might weep day and night for the slain of my poor people!
>
> Jeremiah 8:18-9:1 (NRSV)

What is justice? It seems as if we are offered daily reminders of our desperate need for justice. When the chaos of violence and uncertainty strike, we have to dig deep and ask very hard questions about what justice means and what justice entails, not simply on behalf of those who have wronged us, but for ourselves as well. For in spite of our unruly American character, we at least pride ourselves of being a nation of laws. Justice is one of those good and noble ends to which we as a people aspire, and throughout our two-hundred and twenty-seven-year history under the American Constitution, we have sought to fashion our legal system in pursuit of those ideals. One might say that justice serves as a guiding principle, and as people of faith we believe wholeheartedly that our national system of justice should be a reflection of God's justice. This is why we swear people in the courtroom through the act of laying one's hand upon the bible as we declare, "So help me God", at least symbolizing our belief that the concept of justice derives from a higher power…a divine calling to which we as a nation endeavor to reply.

Go ahead and wander into almost any courtroom in our nation, and you will see her standing somewhere nearby—a set of scales clasped firmly in one hand with sword cradled in the other, blindfold draped over her eyes, wholly symmetrical features, elegant flowing robes which appear to defy the very stone from which she is cleft, or the iron from which she is wrought. It's no accident men throughout history have sought to personify justice in a form which they yearn for—an idealized embodiment which entices and beckons our very being. And there upon her perch she keeps her guard…constant, vigilant, unwavering, unyielding, unbiased…*perfect*… everything we could possibly desire!

But as the saying goes, she's way out of your league, buddy. Frequently, the human application of justice pales in comparison to this ideal which we have manufactured for ourselves. Who exactly is justice, anyway? Is her goal to punish, or to protect? Does she chastise, or correct? Is she there for revenge, or rehabilitation? Well, that all depends on who you ask. To my knowledge, I don't think we as a nation have ever arrived at any sort of consensus over such questions. So, in order to compensate for this mystery, we have a tendency to project. We project our personal needs upon her, so that justice appears to us, not as who she actually is, but more like who we want her to be.

We are all aware that there is something within our human nature that desires justice in all her forms. We are all familiar with that warm glow we get inside of our hearts when we hear that guilty verdict come down, or when the corrupt become undone as a consequence of their own scheming. We feel a certain satisfaction when the serial rapist gets murdered in prison or when we see oppressed peoples storming the gates of their dictator. When we witness such events in the news or society, we feel a sense of sublime satisfaction that justice is indeed there for us— the world is as it should be when the wrath of an angry God is at hand. However, in spite of appearances, this is not who we might think. We have a nasty habit of confusing justice with her many siblings. She might be ironic, she might even be poetic, but justice she is not!

After all, how can we recognize justice…how can we comprehend what justice requires, when we never even taken the time to get to know her in the first place? How can you truly understand who she is, and what her needs are, when all we ever did was simply flirt with her to begin with? Where is the commitment? Where is the fidelity? Where is the sense of obligation? At what point did we assume that justice was simply there to provide us with a sense of personal fulfillment by which our short-term emotional needs are satisfied? What a low opinion we must have of her, if we believe that she would somehow be content with such a superficial and casual relationship!

"For the LORD is a God of justice…" declares the prophet Isaiah [30:18]. Isaiah proclaimed the Word of the Lord in a very different time than that of Jeremiah. When Isaiah was active and at work in the southern kingdom of Judah, there was still hope—there was still the possibility that the twin Hebrew kingdoms of Israel and Judah could still pull themselves out of the moral tailspin in which they found themselves, turning away from idolatry and selfishness to return to the Lord. Yet by the time the prophet Jeremiah arrives upon the scene a century and a half later, that former hope had dissipated altogether. With Jeremiah, die was now cast, the sentence had been

passed. The Northern Kingdom of Israel had already fallen to their own devices, and all that remained for the people of the Southern Kingdom were the inevitable consequences, by which the kingdom of Jerusalem would collapse, its citizens put to the sword, and those that remained would be defeated and humiliated, sent into exile far from the land of the God's promises. Judah would behold the Lord's justice in all her terrible glory!

And yet even though God's justice would come to pass, even though the people of Judah would deserve everything they would receive as a consequence of their stubborn disobedience to God's will, this would prove no cause for joy, especially in the eyes of the Lord. Indeed, the voice of the Lord spoken through the prophet mourns Jerusalem's fate. *"My joy is gone, grief is upon me, / my heart is sick…For the hurt of my poor people I am hurt, / I mourn, and dismay has taken hold of me."* When justice is served, when sinful and disobedient people, "get what they deserve", when the tables become turned and shoe lies on the other foot, this is not cause for celebration, but lamentation.

This is something to consider in our own pursuit of justice, that justice is unimpressed by petty desires for revenge, righteous indignation or our need for smug satisfaction. Punishment and accountability are sometimes unfortunate, but necessary, components of human justice, but it is hardly cause to celebrate. If anything, when someone finally gets what they deserve, it remains a source of great sadness—sadness for those who shallowly perpetuate such crimes, and sadness for victims who are forced to bear the burden of their severity. Through the prophet Jeremiah, God expresses a tremendous sense of loss when human beings callously exact such violence and disregard upon one another, as we once again invite divine judgment upon us for our failure to be the people who God has intended us to be.

And this may be the single most tragic thing about the many horrors that we inflict upon one another; they cause us to doubt that there is a God out there who loves and cares for us and wants the best for us. Human cruelty forces us into cycles of despair and hopelessness, where we feel little recourse but to give as the world gives, returning violence for violence and injury for injury, wishing reciprocal pain upon those who have wronged us. Such callousness obscures our human potential for goodness while preventing us from seeing the many ways in which the Holy Spirit is present and at work within others.

"The Lord is a God of justice," declares the prophet Isaiah. These were the words which I so righteously echoed to Bill Klein, the pastor of Lexington

Presbyterian Church, one afternoon while immersed in a theological discussion. (Pastors enjoy very long-winded theological discussions. It helps us feel smart and important!) However, Bill quickly and wisely tempered my zeal by pointing out the ways in which our Lord is *not* a God of justice. He mentioned that justice is about getting what you deserve, but as Christians, we know that *we have never actually gotten what we deserve!* Like the people of Judah millennia before, we have failed to live and act as the people of God. We too have allowed people to suffer as a consequence of our greed and selfishness. We have permitted the hungry to go without food and the poor to go without their daily needs. We have turned a blind eye to the suffering of others and a deaf ear to the cries of the oppressed. We pass out judgments and sentences unjustly, which often fall disproportionately upon the most vulnerable among us. We enrich ourselves as others are forced to go without. In the courtroom of God's justice, we all stand convicted. Yet through Jesus Christ we have been forgiven of those many debts of human cruelty to which we owe our Lord. Only by the grace of God, *we do not get what we deserve*, simply because one man was willing to serve the punishment for the sins of many.

Therefore, as God's people, if we assume for a moment that getting what we rightfully deserve would be cause for lamentation, then it stands to reason that the *opposite* might also be true— that NOT getting what we rightfully deserve would be cause for celebration! Even though we are sinners, even though we know that we prove undeserving of the gift of grace which we have so generously received through Jesus Christ, even though we know we may likely fail and fail again, we should not hesitate in our calling to offer thanksgiving to our Lord that we live as *forgiven* people, for it is as such we have been invited to be participants in God's ultimate plan for all creation. Toward this end, the pursuit of justice has a rightful and necessary place among our national priorities, but as a forgiven people, let us not forget for one moment that so do compassion, mercy, reconciliation and love!

Revenge may seem sweet, but she can never be confused with justice. Cycles of revenge and retribution only open wounds, they can never truly repair them. With them we are made less whole, reduced to a mere fraction of our former selves. When we are hurt, or when we feel wronged or when our hearts cry out for justice, very often we crave vengeance first, when what we should actually seek is healing. Through the prophet Jeremiah, the Lord assures God's people that there is indeed a balm in Gilead. Although in the wake of such pain, the prospect of healing may seem very far away, restoration and wholeness can be made real under the guiding hand of our Lord. Through God's grace and mercy, healing is possible, but we can never get there clinging to the twin anchors of hatred and revenge. Such heaviness of heart only weighs us down in the labor of the Good News.

I know that it's quite easy for me to stand and proclaim forgiveness and reconciliation from the safety of this pulpit hundreds, or perhaps even thousands of miles away from tragedy, just as I know that there are no simple answers in the pursuit of the Lord's justice. I know that it is impossible for me to understand the motives of those who would perpetrate harm others in such a cold and careless manner. Yet as resolute as such evil can be, I do know that those who proclaim God's healing love must be at least equally so determined, for the Lord has already shown us which of these is stronger.

Blessing and glory and wisdom and thanksgiving and honor and power and might be to our God forever and ever. Amen.

How does one measure the success of ministry? This is an important question for churches to ask themselves. For decades, we measured the success of a church by a single standard—in terms of numbers, reflected through membership, offerings and attendance—so each denomination felt an urgency to open a new church with each proposed subdivision. No one ever imagined a sustained period of contraction among the churchgoing population. The obvious failures of 20th century growth models are being experienced by Waynesboro and many other communities in our nation; we have a surplus of church buildings with not enough parishioners to fill them. The result is congregations who are property-rich, but resource poor, which requires disproportionate resources to be used in maintaining a physical structure, instead of improving upon mission and outreach in the community. Consolidation would make logical sense, but how do you convince someone to give up the pew where their great-grandparents worshipped, or the font from which their children were baptized? When it comes to people and their churches, one can pretty much take logic and reason and toss them right out the stained-glass window!

What does it mean to be the church? This question which dogged the early apostles has once again brought itself to light, sometimes unnervingly so. And just as we need a new definition for the church for the 21st century, we also require a new measure for success. Don't get me wrong: It is still good to want to grow and to prosper, but we cannot be limited by the math. The people who show up at our doors are not really concerned about whether the worship service is contemporary or traditional, or over the political or social leanings of the pastor or denomination. Without exception, ALL the people who have joined our congregation during my tenure have expressed a sincere desire to become involved in both church and community. Success for the church means providing those opportunities. I think, above all things, in this impersonal and subjective age in which we live, people crave authenticity above all else, and authenticity can arrive in a variety of forms, not just one. Success comes from being true to ourselves as disciples of Jesus Christ, and servants of the Most High God.

(Whoever catches the Monty Python reference first wins!)

No Man's Land

11 On the way to Jerusalem Jesus was going through the region between Samaria and Galilee. 12As he entered a village, ten lepers approached him. Keeping their distance, 13they called out, saying, 'Jesus, Master, have mercy on us!' 14When he saw them, he said to them, 'Go and show yourselves to the priests.' And as they went, they were made clean.

> *¹⁵Then one of them, when he saw that he was healed, turned back, praising God with a loud voice. ¹⁶He prostrated himself at Jesus' feet and thanked him. And he was a Samaritan. ¹⁷Then Jesus asked, 'Were not ten made clean? But the other nine, where are they? ¹⁸Was none of them found to return and give praise to God except this foreigner?' ¹⁹Then he said to him, 'Get up and go on your way; your faith has made you well.'*
>
> Luke 17:11-19 (NRSV)

In our passage today, Jesus is on a mission. In Luke's gospel, it has been eight chapters since Jesus first, *"set his face toward Jerusalem"* [9:51] to begin his final journey to the cross, and now he and his disciples find themselves in an unnamed place, somewhere, "through the region between Samaria and Galilee." Normally, Jesus travelling abroad wouldn't strike us as odd, but then we think to ourselves, "Wait a minute…isn't Samaria where this journey began? You mean to tell me that after all this time we're no closer than when we started?" It would appear as if Jesus and his disciples have spent the previous eight chapters literally wandering around in circles! It seems unclear if they even know where they are, much less where they're going. According to Luke, their exact location is ambiguous; they are not in Samaria, nor are they in Galilee; they are neither here nor there, but somewhere in between.

And within this odd, unnamed place, a strange encounter takes place. Jesus and his disciples are approached a group of ten lepers. These lepers appear to be just as ambiguous as the land which they occupy. The severity of their disease has disfigured all evidence of their ethnic or religious origins. We are unable to tell if they are from Samaritan lands to the north or the Jewish lands of Galilee to the east. Ancient animosities are forgotten as they suffer from a common affliction. Regardless of where they originated, because of the uncleanliness of their disease, each one has been forced to live in exile within this obscure region in between their respective communities. In every sense, these ten are the forgotten nameless, faceless mob of lepers who exist neither here nor there, but somewhere in between.

Throughout the centuries, Christians have come to perceive the church as performing a largely *social* function—that it is the church's responsibility to minister to those living within its bounds. Often we uphold the individual congregation as a community in and of ourselves, and as a result, Christian mission has a tendency to focus inward directed to those causes which we feel most comfortable with, and those things that have the most direct impact on our day-today lives. Mission serves as a reflection the priorities of a particular congregation, and more often than not, our first priority is ourselves.

Of course, there is certainly nothing wrong with looking after the needs of your particular congregation; in many ways this is why we gather together once a week the way we do, to take stock of our church family to discover where our present needs are. But this episode from the Gospel of Luke reminds us that the aim of mission is not solely to look inward toward our respective needs, but rather it is our calling as Christ's disciples to follow where Jesus leads, journeying to unfamiliar places to minister to those who exist out upon the margins, outside of our comfort zone. By his example, Jesus reminds us that we must broaden our vision to see the forgotten and the marginalized among us, people whose need is so great that it obscures their faces and identities, rendering them unrecognizable and thereby that much easier to ignore.

As Christ enters into this obscure village, the group of ten cries out to Jesus from a distance saying, "*Jesus, Master, have mercy upon us!*" Upon hearing their cries, Christ does not bother to ask this group of lepers who they are, nor does he ask them where they come from or how deserving they may be or which faith they profess. He doesn't issue a "means test" to make sure that they are actually who they say they are. No…when he hears the cries of people in need, Christ's first instinct is to respond *immediately*, and all are made clean. This disease which defined them simply fades away, and as a consequence, they are all able to return to the communities from which they came. Their identity and humanity become restored through Jesus Christ, and these former lepers are now able to reclaim that which their affliction had taken away.

This gets to the heart of what Christian mission should be about. The purpose of mission is not only to help and to heal, but its aim should also be to restore. This means looking beyond statistics and beyond differences to recognize the humanity we share in common. Mission should acknowledge how a person in need is a person just like us, and but for chance or fortune, we could just as easily be on the outside looking in. Mission shouldn't exist just to give away a free meal, donate to charity or provide medical care and then send people on their merry way, but with equal emphasis the goal of Christian mission should be to erase those mental and physical divides that isolate us from one another—to not merely label persons as "the poor" or "the hungry" or "the sick". Such distinctions, no matter how well intended, only serve to obscure the humanity of people in need. If we relieve someone of their affliction, yet fail to embrace them back into community, then we've only done our job halfway!

Returning to our story for a moment, in a strange way, something becomes lost when Jesus heals these ten lepers. These people no doubt came from different lands, different peoples, and yet here they are, united by their common frailty. In many ways, it was their shared brokenness which brought these ten together. Now that they have been restored, now that they no longer have this sickness in common with one another, they quickly disperse back to their native communities. Some would undoubtedly go north to the priests in Samaria, while others would return south to Judah where they would easily slip back into former habits, renewing longstanding hatreds and grudges, clinging to the same tired ways, with the memory of their collective isolation wiped away in an instant as if nothing had ever happened. Indeed, if they ever encountered one of their former compatriots again, it may likely be as an enemy. These ten lepers were healed in the hope that they might become part of a new community, that former ways and old hatreds would be forgotten and that they would gather together once again, this time as followers of Jesus Christ. And yet the vast majority of these former lepers would turn their backs on him. I guess there's no pleasing some people.

As these lepers disperse to return to their homes, a strange episode soon follows. One man— only one man—turns back and comes before Jesus in gratitude, praising God *"with a loud voice."* Now that disease no longer defines who he is, now that he is invisible and untouchable no longer, we can tell that he is a Samaritan. This man prostrates himself before Jesus, thanking him for all he had done, and seeing him there alone, Jesus asks, *"Were not ten made clean? But the other nine, where are they? Was none of them found to return and give praise to God except this foreigner?"* Thus, witnessing this lone man before him, Jesus declares, *"Get up and go on your way; your faith has made you well."*

Upon hearing this story, the first instinct of the listener is usually righteous indignation. Most commentaries that I read oversimplify the moral of the story as, "Ten are healed, but only one is saved," and simply leave it as such. Listeners hear this and think to themselves, "One out of ten…really? Jesus does this amazing thing for these people in need and only one in ten comes back to say thank you? One in *ten*? How awful!" However, when pastors hear this story, they think to themselves, "One out of ten…really? That's *amazing*! Now that truly is a miracle!" So many aspects of ministry fall within vague abstractions of religion and spirituality, there is often little *tangible* measure by which one can gauge success. Too often it can seem as if we too are merely running around in circles in a theological no man's land, and we can never really tell whether or not we are actually making any progress proclaiming the Good News.

Luke's gospel underscores how true Christian mission is difficult, unrewarding and often goes unappreciated, so therefore, to have one person in ten to come forward and offer gratitude and praise to God is actually, when you think about it, quite an impressive feat. After all, Jesus was the divine Logos incarnate, fully human and fully divine, a man in whom the fullness of God was pleased to dwell. He raised the dead and healed the sick and performed signs and wonders for all to see, and yet the best the Son of Man could do was one out of ten! Thus, we can begin to appreciate the many frustrations associated with Christian mission, because Christ experienced them too! And if ten percent is the best Jesus can do, what hope is there for the rest of us?

Whereas ten percent may be good odds for ministry, it's bad odds for Vegas. And people never like to take chances when it comes to matters of faith; we want a sure thing, preferring certainty over trust. So, in order to improve our odds, we could easily do what many churches and denominations do and adopt an incentive program for people to come to Jesus Christ, declaring, "*If* you believe, *then* you will be healed." "*If* you have enough faith, *then* you will be made whole!" "*If* you can do a little something for us, *then* you will be rewarded!" Such ideas serve as a poor excuse for evangelism, for it is not our place to impose conditions on the grace of God. Our sole mission as Christ's disciples is to share generously and abundantly—and whoever comes will come, and whoever won't will not. Our focus needs to be upon the things we can control, instead of the things we cannot. Through the generous sharing of the Spirit, our hope is that others will be able to recognize the Spirit acting within themselves. Because if we prove unwilling to act like Christ's church, then we can't really expect them to either…

Of course, recognition of our efforts in mission is a wonderful blessing, and in many ways, reaching that one person makes all of the frustrations worthwhile. But that's not why we do it. We do not do these things in the vain hope of converting the unbeliever; we do these difficult and unappreciated things because of a debt we owe. We do these things because know how we too are united by brokenness. We all suffer from the same disease. And yet, Christ found us by the roadside and healed us of our affliction, relieving us of the sinfulness which cripples and distorts our humanity. Only by grace are we able to reclaim our identity as God's people, and we become restored to a community of faith—a *new* community where the pains of the past fade into nothingness. Christian mission is the means by which we approach our Lord to express gratitude, and even if it just happens ten percent of the time—well, that's still pretty good in my book. And as God has given to us, so are we to give to one another—generously, abundantly, freely and without condition, with the love and hope of Jesus Christ being our only reward. We have been called by name to serve one another by name. Only by caring for others can we truly rediscover our own humanity.

Blessing and glory and wisdom and thanksgiving and honor and power and might be to our God forever and ever. Amen.

www.ingramcontent.com/pod-product-compliance
Lightning Source LLC
Chambersburg PA
CBHW071621080526
44588CB00010B/1213